UNDER *His* INFLUENCE

Yielding TO THE WORK OF THE *Holy Spirit*

BY LLOYD PULLEY

DEDICATION

I would like to dedicate this book to a wrestler who was on the wrestling team at Michigan State University with me in the fall of 1976. Although his name escapes me today, his life and testimony have left a lasting impression. His example not only sparked in me a desire to be a Christian, but also helped me to understand how to live a life that was yielded to, and empowered by the Holy Spirit.

ACKNOWLEDGMENTS

No one finishes a project like this without the support and encouragement of others. I am especially blessed to have had the input of so many trusted and talented friends and staff who took time out of their busy schedules to review and critique the early manuscript (you know who you are). Your heart for God and commitment to excellence marked this book with much more than red ink.

I would like to thank the staff at Calvary Chapel Publishing. What a great team with whom to work. You truly are our family in Christ.

I would also like to thank the faithful servants in Calvary Chapel Old Bridge's publications ministry who labored behind the scenes to help bring this book to life. Your attention to the small details like grammar, spelling, clarity, and complete sentences have made all the difference. You know I couldn't have done it without you.

Special thanks to Arlene Solomon who envisioned and wrote the study guide for this book.

A very special thanks to Noreen Hay who labored abundantly, transforming my thoughts, scribbles, and words into an easy-to-read manuscript. Without you this book would never have come forth.

And, of course, to my precious wife Karen, who knows all too well when I am NOT yielded "under His influence," but is patient to wait for the grace of God to convict me and move me toward Him.

Most of all, to my Lord, who knows me perfectly, has borne me up when I have been down, and has guided me faithfully. May this book be an encouragement to Your people!

TABLE OF CONTENTS

◆ ◆ ◆

ESTABLISHING A CONNECTION

Do you ever find yourself lacking power to live the Christian life? I heard a story once about a missionary who was given a car to use while staying in a foreign country. Although he was grateful for the convenience, there was one problem. He was not able to start the engine without using jumper cables. This became a nuisance, so he devised a clever way to start the car without needing any help. Wherever he went, he would make sure he was parked on a hill. He would then be able to start the car by letting it roll down the hill. As it rolled, he would pop the clutch, start the engine, and be on his way. That was how he kept the car running for the two years that he was in that country.

However, just before he was due to leave, he was explaining the process to another missionary who would now be using the car. As he was speaking, the other guy decided to look under the hood. "Hey wait a minute," he said, "looks like there's a loose connection here. I wonder if this has anything to do with the problem?" He gave it a twist, got in the car, and the engine started without any trouble. The problem was resolved as soon as the connection to the source of power was established.

This story has a great spiritual application. Sometimes we tend to keep our Christian lives going just like this missionary kept his car running: by depending on our own human ingenuity instead of simply making sure we are connected to our source of power. If you have become worn out trying to keep your engine running lately, perhaps, like this missionary discovered, the problem is simply a loose connection.

PLEASING GOD

When I was four years old, my mother died, and my grandmother took over the job of raising my sisters and me. When I was around five years old, I remember saying to my grandmother as she was watching Billy Graham on television, "Grandma, when I grow up, I'm gonna be just like him." That's easy to say when you are five years old, but by the time I was a teenager, I had experienced a definite change of heart. I decided that being a Christian was just *too* hard, and that those who said they were Christians were really hypocrites. They had to be, because there was no way that anyone could ever really live a life that was good enough to please God!

So I walked away from Christianity and sought after other philosophies, looking for anything that would make me happy. But nothing ever did. And of course, I could never get away from my grandma's prayers. I used to ask her to stop praying for me (she was ruining all my fun), but thankfully, she never did.

Later, when I was on the wrestling team in college, I learned that one of my fellow wrestlers was a Christian. I noticed something very different about him though—he had the ability to actually live the Christian life. As I watched him, I saw that he had joy, integrity, and a lifestyle that really reflected the qualities of Christ. It was so appealing to me that I wanted what he had, so I asked him, "What's your secret?"

What I learned from him was life changing. It was something that was simple to understand, yet powerful when applied, and it was something I had never known before. I learned that the key to living as a Christian is really a Person—the Person of the Holy Spirit who dwells in us and wants to empower us in our Christian walk. What I realized was that it was not that I *lacked* the power to live a life that is pleasing to God, but, like the missionary with the loose wires, I needed to be connected to the Source—the Holy Spirit.

When I finally understood the connection between the Holy Spirit and my ability to live a victorious Christian life, I recognized that what I needed to do was yield my life to His control every day. Trying to live the Christian life apart from the empowerment of the Holy Spirit is bondage.

I found that as I began to yield the control of my life to Him on a daily basis, I had the power to do what I was not able to do before. I had the power to resist temptation and sin, to understand the Scriptures, to enjoy prayer, and to share my faith with others. I had joy and peace, and the power to live above my circumstances. As I learned to yield to the Holy Spirit, I discovered how freeing it really is to be a Christian!

As a pastor today, it grieves me to see the number of Christians, even in my own fellowship, who are still caught in the bondage of trying to live the Christian life in their own strength—or, worse yet, those who have given up trying altogether and have settled for a life of compromise and backsliding.

That is why I wanted to write this book. It was not written to replace other fine books on the subject of the Holy Spirit, but rather to add something to the discussion, especially in the area of practical Christian living. What I hope to do here is to help Christians bridge the gap between what we know (theologically) and what we actually do (practically) in our daily lives. Christians need to understand the incredible resource that we have been given in the Holy Spirit and how He can empower our lives on a continual basis. Does that mean that each of us will fully grasp this knowledge and apply it perfectly in our lives? No, but as we choose to yield to the influence of the Holy Spirit, we will experience a dramatic difference in the way we live. We will become more like Jesus, who perfectly exemplified the power of a life lived under the influence of the Holy Spirit.

HIS LIFE IN US

When God created man in Genesis 2:7, we read how He *"breathed into his nostrils the breath of life; and man became a living being."* The Holy Spirit was first given to the disciples in a similar way. After the resurrection, Jesus met with them, and in John 20:22 we learn that He *"breathed on them, and said to them, 'Receive the Holy Spirit.'"* It appears that at that point, they were born again and filled with the Spirit. The Holy Spirit was now dwelling in them.

However, on the day Jesus ascended into heaven He commanded these same disciples to wait in Jerusalem for the power of the Holy Spirit to *"come upon"* them (Acts 1:4–8). Ten days later, on the day of Pentecost (Acts 2), the Holy Spirit came upon those believers, empowering them to be His witnesses. Indeed, we read throughout the book of Acts how the Holy Spirit came upon them on several occasions as they waited on Him and yielded their lives wholly to His leading.

So, the disciples first received the Holy Spirit when they were born again. And as they continued to *yield* their lives to Him, they were empowered and refreshed on numerous occasions. What we learn about the ministry of the Holy Spirit, therefore, is that believers can, and should, expect to have more than one experience with Him. This is the way the Holy Spirit works in the life of a yielded Christian.

Scripture clearly reveals the distinction and correlation between what God does in *filling* us with His Spirit and what we do in being *yielded* to Him on a daily basis. One good example of this relationship is found in the life of Stephen, the first Christian who was killed for his faith. Scripture reveals that he was:

1. *"A man **full** of faith and the Holy Spirit . . ."* (Acts 6:5, emphasis added).

2. *"[A man who] being **full** of the Holy Spirit, gazed into heaven and saw the glory of God, and Jesus standing at the right hand of God!"* (Acts 7:55, emphasis added).

These verses tell us, similarly, that Stephen was a man who was *full* of the Spirit of God. Yet, we can see a clear distinction being made as we look at the context of these verses. For instance, in the first reference, being full of the Spirit refers to his daily demeanor. However, what we see in the second reference in Acts 7:55 is a little different. Here we see how Stephen, being full of the Spirit, yields his life to the Lord. And, in his final hours, he literally gazes *into* heaven and is strengthened by the very Presence of God. It was a move of the Spirit upon his life, empowering him with the faith that he needed at that moment to stand as a witness for Christ.

Just as the Holy Spirit came upon Stephen and those early believers in the book of Acts, He will also come upon each of us as we daily yield our lives to Him. The problem is that many of us are looking for something different. We are looking for a particular experience or feeling to trust in, rather than simply being willing to yield to His Presence. However, being yielded is the key to being filled with the Holy Spirit.

Paul instructed the Ephesian church regarding the necessity of being yielded to the Spirit. In Ephesians 5:18 he said to them, *"Be filled with the Spirit."* An even better rendering of this verse would be, "Be *continually* filled with the Spirit," because the emphasis in the original language is on our present and ongoing need for the continual filling of the Holy Spirit. The point Paul is making is that this is something *we* must do. But, practically speaking, how do we do this? How do we remain filled with the Holy Spirit?

OUR PART IS TO YIELD

The answer is simple: we need to recognize His authority over us by submitting to His leading and continually posturing ourselves in a position where we need His power. When we do this, we are making ourselves available to be used by God as He chooses. Ultimately, it is not for us to decide the way in which He will use our lives. That is His part. Our part is to be yielded and available, willing to follow wherever He leads.

At times, God's leading in our lives is very subtle. In His sovereignty, He unfolds His plans through ordinary circumstances. Chuck Smith, the senior pastor of Calvary Chapel of Costa Mesa, once told of how God had used something as natural as his appetite in order to lead him to an opportunity to minister. I remember Chuck sharing how all he wanted was a burrito, but God had another idea. (That kind of thing always happens to me at Starbucks!) When we are yielded to the Holy Spirit, God can pencil in His divine appointments on our busy calendars. The point is: when we are yielded to the Spirit, He folds the seemingly mundane, everyday decisions that we make into His divine design for our lives.

Ultimately, it is not for us to decide the way in which He will use our lives. That is His part. Our part is to be yielded and available, willing to follow wherever He leads.

Indeed, as we are sensitive to the Spirit and available for His purposes, the Lord can and will lead us each day. But we need to be careful of being presumptuous. Presumption is when we assign God's purposes to our own thoughts and plans. For instance, I remember as a young Christian, I wanted to be led by God more than anything else. I would try so hard to listen for His voice. Then one day, as I was driving on the freeway, I thought I sensed the Lord telling me to get off at a particular exit. So I got off. And said, "Okay, Lord, which way should I go now?" I was sensing that He was directing me to "go left" at one corner, then "right" at the next. I drove around in circles like that for hours until I realized that I was not following God's voice at all, just my own thoughts.

I can laugh at this now, but at the time I thought it was my job "to figure out" the Lord's leading in my life, and that was very confusing. However, what I continue to learn is that if I desire to be led of the Lord, I must simply choose to be yielded to Him. When I am, He is able to lead me without me even realizing it. When my life is yielded to His, I can rest assured, knowing that I am always in the center of His will for me.

The following pages were written to help Christians understand the importance of living lives yielded to the influence of the Holy Spirit. My heart's desire is that we would rise to this challenge and begin to apply ourselves fully and with all diligence to the calling that God has on our lives so that His perfect will would be accomplished in and through us. My hope is that this book would provide practical teaching and a timely exhortation on the necessity and simplicity of being yielded to, and led by, the Spirit of God. My prayer is that it would help Christians, no matter where we are in our walk with the Lord, to:

1. Know the kind of Christian life we can live.

2. Understand who the Holy Spirit is and how He works in us.

3. Learn how to be and remain filled with the Spirit.

4. Experience the bountiful, overflowing life that is ours in Christ.

5. Be able to discern the truth, walk in victory, and experience personal revival.

6. See Jesus alive and moving in our lives.

Paul's injunction in Ephesians 5:18 is that we would be filled "continually" with the Spirit of God. As I write this book, that desire is in my heart too. I pray that all who read this would be filled with the Spirit of God. After all, why would we want to live an empty Christian life when we can be filled with the dynamic, transforming power of God? Why would we want the world to see us when they could see Jesus in us instead? That is the life that God has designed for all who willingly choose to live *Under His Influence.*

Introduction Study Guide

ESTABLISHING A CONNECTION

◆ ◆ ◆

1. Why did you decide to read a book about living under the influence of the Holy Spirit? What do you hope to learn from reading this book?

   _____

   _____

   _____

2. Do you think being a Christian is too hard? Explain.

   _____

   _____

   _____

3. Do you know someone whose life is a demonstration of the power of the Holy Spirit? Write one thing about their life that would draw others to Christ.

   _____

   _____

   _____

4. What is the key to living as a Christian, and what is the main problem that prevents many Christians from being able to live for Christ?

   _____

   _____

5. Trying to live the Christian life apart from the empowerment of the Holy Spirit is _____. Why?

_____

_____

6. Fill in the blanks to this quote taken from the *Introduction.*

   "[This book has been written to] help Christians bridge the gap between what we know _____ and what we actually do _____ in our daily lives."

7. Now answer this question: Is your daily life a demonstration of the theology that you profess? Why or why not?

_____

_____

8. Why do you think Paul commanded the Ephesian church to *"be filled with the Spirit"* (Ephesians 5:18)? Draw on anything you might know about the church in Ephesus at that time.

_____

_____

9. What is our part in being filled with the Spirit?

_____

_____

Paul's injunction to all believers is to be filled with the Spirit of God. Write your prayer asking the Lord to instruct and teach you how to live *Under His Influence.*

_____

_____

_____

The Master's plan, and what a genius of a plan it is—is this, that the world should be won, not by the preachers—though we must have these men of God for leadership—but by everyone who knows the story of Jesus telling someone, and telling not only with his lips earnestly and tactfully, but even more, telling with his life. This is the Master's plan . . . and it makes a great difference to Him and to the world outside whether you and I are living the story of His love and power among men or not.[1]

—*S. D. Gordon*

WHAT KIND OF CHRISTIAN ARE YOU?

When my daughter was about seven years old, I remember putting her to bed one night after reading the story of how Jesus calmed the storm by commanding the waves to *"be still"* (Mark 4:39). As we prayed, she let out a little sigh and said, "It's not fair! The disciples got to see Jesus and we don't get to see Him."

I began to explain to her, in a way that I hoped she could understand, why it was that Jesus had to go away. I said, "Honey, imagine what it would be like if Jesus were still on earth as a man today. We think that would be great, right? We could just go right up to Him, like the disciples did, with any question or problem and He would take care of it for us. But really, we wouldn't be able to spend that much time with Him at all. We wouldn't be able to get to know Him because there would be such a long line of people waiting to see Him; we would only be able to say a few words and that would be it. That's why Jesus said it was better that He go away, so that the Holy Spirit could come and live with all those who believe in Him."

In His humanity, Jesus' ministry was limited. You can do the math on this yourself. If you divide the five billion-plus people in the world today by the thirty years of Jesus' earthly life, each of us would get less than half-a-second to spend with Him. What kind of an impact could He really make on our lives in such a short amount of time? How well could we really get to know Him? Even before we could say, "Hello Jesus," our time would be up.

That is why Jesus said that it would be better for us when the Holy Spirit came, and why He took time to speak to His disciples about the ministry of the Holy Spirit before He went to the cross. He wanted them to be comforted in the knowledge that He was not going to be leaving them alone like orphans in this world. He also wanted them to know that it actually would be to their advantage that He went away so that the Holy Spirit could come and remain with them forever. At the time, they could not have possibly understood the fullness of what He was saying, but He told them anyway, so that later on they would remember how Jesus had promised to send the Holy Spirit to them.

The indwelling Presence and empowerment of the Holy Spirit in the life of a believer is the basis of the Christian life. Charles Spurgeon once said,

> As breath is the very life of the physical man, so the Spirit of God is the life of the spiritual man. By Him were we reborn at the first; by Him our spiritual life is sustained; by Him is the inner life nurtured, increased and perfected.[2]

Many Christians who attend church on a regular basis look pretty good on the outside, yet when you get a little closer, you realize that they are missing something. They do not seem to have this inner blessing. It is evident by the lack of power they have to change the way that they are living. They are enslaved to bad attitudes, passions, and habitual sins. And, they are not truly experiencing, firsthand, the power of God in their lives.

In his day, the apostle Paul reminded the Corinthians that their lives were living epistles, *"known and read by all men"* (2 Corinthians 3:2). That is a good reminder for the church today as well. What would others "know and read" of our lives if they were to look closely at the way we are living? Would they see Jesus in us? Would they read the story of His grace and power in the chapters of our lives? Or, would they be surprised to find out that we are Christians at all?

Indeed, as Christians, you and I ought to be living out the story of Jesus' grace, love, and power everywhere we go. But does the thought of that overwhelm you and make you feel like you are on a "Christian treadmill" at times? Are you being worn out trying to live up to the holy standards of others, or possibly even your own? Or, has the Christian life simply become too lofty an ideal to maintain on a daily basis?

I used to feel many of those same things myself as a young person growing up in a Christian home. I remember that the focus of my Christianity at that time was always on what I could do (or should do) for God. And, of course, I was never able to live up to such high expectations. No one ever told me that the power I needed to live a life that was pleasing to God was available if I would just yield my life to the Holy Spirit. So I began to think that being a Christian was just too hard. And really, I was not too far from the truth—without the help of the Holy Spirit, being a Christian *is* too hard.

> Without the help of the Holy Spirit, being a Christian *is* too hard.

The good news is this: in the Holy Spirit we have an unlimited resource who enables us to live the Christian life. God never intended for us to wear ourselves out. He simply wants us to believe and be completely dependent upon the Holy Spirit. He wants us to trust Him to lead us, to guide us, and to let Him be Lord over every aspect of our lives and every hidden corner of our hearts. Wherever the world has scarred us, or whatever has caused us to faint, no matter what sin has gripped us in the past—His life *in us* will redeem it all. His grace is sufficient, His sacrifice is complete, and if we let Him, He will unfold, with each passing day, the beautiful story that He has authored for our lives.

ABIDING IN HIM

Wherever we are in our walks with the Lord today, there is no doubt that God can do even more—more than we can possibly imagine. However, only through a continual, intimate, and abiding relationship with the Holy Spirit will we be able to go forward each day in *His* strength. Abiding in Him is not a work that we have to do in order to please God. As a matter of fact, it is just the opposite. Abiding is actually coming to an end of all our own efforts at living the Christian life. To *abide* literally means "to dwell with permanently," "to continue," or "to remain under." Therefore, an intimate and abiding relationship with the Lord is found as we simply spend time with Him in daily fellowship—dwelling in His Presence and feasting in His Word. This is our spiritual nourishment; it is our daily bread.

Abiding is actually coming to an end of all our own efforts at living the Christian life.

A good illustration of this type of abiding relationship is found in the Old Testament book of Exodus. In chapter 16, we read that God was providing heavenly manna each day to sustain His people in the wilderness. He had instructed Moses to have them collect only enough to meet their daily needs. As long as they did, they never experienced any lack; they had enough manna for that day. However, some of them grew tired of the daily manna routine, so they came up with what they thought was a better plan. They decided to gather enough manna for two days instead of one as the Lord had instructed. But to their surprise, the next morning they found that their day-old manna was of no use to them. It was full of worms! Their cleverness had cost them their nourishment that day; their human ingenuity had only served to weaken them.

The lack that resulted as a consequence of not following God's plan is a great picture of what happens to us, spiritually speaking, when we grow tired of God's ways. Just as the children in the wilderness could not be sustained by their day-old heavenly food, neither can we. The time we spend alone in His Word and in prayerful communion with Him is how we gather our "manna" every day. He is our *"Bread of Life,"* and it is His life that is the source of our spiritual strength. Without the fresh manna found in the Word of God each day, we too will grow weak. As we abide in Him, He sustains us through His Word and empowers us by His Spirit to live for Him no matter what comes our way.

THE POWER OF THE HOLY SPIRIT

D. L. Moody once said,

> You might as well try to hear without ears, or breathe without lungs, as try to live a Christian life without the Spirit of God in your heart.[3]

We miss the point when we fail to recognize that the only power we have to live the Christian life is found in the Holy Spirit. It is not so much that we receive power from Him as it is that we receive His very life in us—His infinite resources and abilities in our finite lives. As the apostle Paul said, *"We have this treasure in earthen vessels, that the excellence of the power may be of God and not of us"* (2 Corinthians 4:7). Through the Holy Spirit's indwelling Presence, we are able to live as God intended. Our lives can only become holy and set apart for His purposes as we yield them to the Spirit of God within.

Jesus understands the enormity of our powerlessness. That is why He told His disciples to wait in Jerusalem, saying, *"You shall receive power when the Holy Spirit has come upon you; and you shall be witnesses to Me"* (Acts 1:8). In the original text, the Greek word that is translated "power" in this verse is *dunamis*, which literally means "ability" or "capacity." We will experience a marked increase in our abilities and capacities when we are empowered by the Holy Spirit. The word *dynamite* is also derived from that same Greek word. I especially like that word picture because it gives us a dramatic idea of the enormous power that the Holy Spirit desires to bring into our lives. For instance, if I lit a stick of dynamite and tossed it into a nicely furnished room, would it remain the same afterward? No, of course not. The unleashed power of the dynamite would make a significant difference to the layout of that room.

Now, of course, the Holy Spirit is not a destructive force like dynamite can be, but He is powerful. He makes a significant difference in the layout of our lives. He comes alongside our minds, for example, and He expands our reasoning capacity. He helps us to discern things that we would otherwise miss. He gives us the ability to understand and the wisdom to know how to make the right choices. He helps us to really love others and deny ourselves. He gives us everything we need to live for Him. As the apostle Peter says, *His divine power has given to us all things that pertain to life and godliness* (2 Peter 1:3). We have been given the power of the Holy Spirit so that we will be His witnesses in this world. That takes quite a lot of power, and that is why He instructed His disciples to wait expectantly and to be dependent on nothing less than the dynamic transforming power that He would unleash in their lives through the Person of the Holy Spirit.

> "Not by might nor by power, but by My Spirit," says the LORD of hosts.
>
> —ZECHARIAH 4:6

We need the same power to live as His witnesses today. It takes power not to compromise in the work place. It takes power to stay faithful in marriage. It takes power to turn our eyes away from temptation, especially when no one is watching. It takes power to say no to sin, to put down that destructive habit, to tell the truth even when it hurts, or to put the needs of others before our own. It takes power to forgive, to love, to be kind, to be quiet, to stay pure (both in body and in mind). It takes power to order our steps and not allow the busyness of life to steal time away from what is most important—our personal relationships with the Lord. It takes power to stay close to His heart through the Word and prayer. It takes the power of the Holy Spirit to

> "Not by might nor by power, but by My Spirit," says the LORD of hosts.
> —ZECHARIAH 4:6

live as His witnesses in this world. As the words of an old stanza by Ada R. Habershon so clearly express:

> *I need to be filled for the home-life,*
> *I need it for work outside,*
> *I need it alone in God's presence,*
> *That I may in Him abide.*
>
> *I need to be filled with the Spirit,*
> *To hear or to read His Word,*
> *I need to be filled when by speaking,*
> *I witness for Christ my Lord.*[4]

IS JESUS STICKING OUT ALL OVER?

Jesus' life is a perfect example of a life lived under the influence of the Holy Spirit. Even though He was fully God, He was also fully man. He took on humanity and identified with us in all ways in order to save us. Christ's life, therefore, is a demonstration of the awesome power of the indwelling Holy Spirit, and now by receiving His life in us, we are able to live as Christ did in this world.

I once heard a story about a little girl who learned in Sunday school that God lives inside all of His children. She was thinking about this on the ride home from church and asked her mother if it was true. Her mother, happy to hear that her little girl had been paying attention, said, "Yes honey, that's right. Jesus lives in our hearts." To that the little girl replied, "But mommy, how does He fit in there? God is so big, and if He lives inside us, wouldn't He be sticking out all over?"

It takes power to say no to sin, to put down that destructive habit, to tell the truth even when it hurts, or to put the needs of others before our own.

What a great observation. Indeed, if He is living within us, He should be sticking out all over! So why is it that He is not a more obvious Presence within the church today? The answer is simple: God allows each of us the freedom to choose whether or not we will yield to His Spirit. It is our choice every day and in every circumstance. The question is: Are we willing to allow Him to have His way in our lives?

In high school, I learned at least one important lesson. I was a very successful wrestler at the time, largely due to my coach's influence. One day in particular, he gave me some prudent advice. I was trying to get down to a lower weight class and had been complaining about how hard it was to qualify in that class. Wisely, my coach never argued with me (it *is* hard to lose weight). He simply said to me, "You know, Lloyd, it comes down to this: Whatever you want the most, that is what you're going to do. If you really want to wrestle at that weight class, then you won't eat too much, and you'll qualify. But if you really want to eat, then that's what you'll do, and you won't be able to wrestle at that weight class. You simply have to make up your mind and do what you want the most."

> The question is: Are we willing to allow Him to have His way in our lives?

What I learned from his instruction was that whether I wrestle or not was really my own choice. And he was absolutely right. I would do whatever I valued the most. I could fight and complain, or I could cheat and sneak food, but in the end I would simply be choosing not to qualify. Instead, I chose to cut the weight because what I wanted most was to wrestle at the lower weight class.

It was a great lesson for me, and it is a principle that we can apply spiritually as well. Every choice that we make reveals what is most important to us. These are the days that God has ordained for us to live for Him. Now is our chance to qualify in His weight class! All He asks is that we would be willing. So, what do you want the most? Is it to live for Jesus? Or does something else have a hold of your heart? The answers can only be found by honestly evaluating the way you are living your life. Ask yourself:

- Am I abiding in the Lord, through His Word and prayer?

- Am I developing a deeper desire for the things of God?

- Am I filled, and being filled, with the Spirit?

- Am I seeing His power being demonstrated in my daily life?

- Am I experiencing victory over sin and temptation?

- Am I willingly yielding my life to His every day?

Very simply, the Lord will never force His will upon us. We must bend our wills to His. Essentially, that is what it means to yield. It means that we give the right of way to another (in this case, the Holy Spirit). In the book of Acts, it was said that the disciples *"turned the world upside down"* (Acts 17:6). What an incredible testimony to the power of God in their lives. Can the same be said of you today? Have you turned your world upside down lately—or has the world gotten you turned around instead?

In summary, I believe the reason that we are not seeing more evidence of the Holy Spirit's power at work in the church today is twofold: Christians either lack the knowledge of what the Bible teaches about who the Holy Spirit is and what His rightful place is in our lives, or else, we have chosen to allow the lesser things in life to have a greater influence over us than the Holy Spirit does. In other words, many of us are either unaware of His Presence or unwilling to yield to His Lordship. Those themes will be unfolded throughout this book. But before going on, I want you to honestly consider how you are living your life. Do you realize the power available *in you* to live for Christ, or have you become content to settle for a mediocre Christian experience? I promise you this: God can pour His Spirit out upon you and revive you. He can turn your world upside down if you would just trust in Him alone and yield your life to His purposes.

> In the book of Acts, it was said that the disciples *"turned the world upside down." . . .* Can the same be said of you today?

I beseech you therefore, brethren, by the mercies of God, that you present your bodies a living sacrifice, holy, acceptable to God, which is your reasonable service. And do not be conformed to this world, but be transformed by the renewing of your mind, that you may prove what is that good and acceptable and perfect will of God.

—ROMANS 12:1–2

Chapter One Study Guide

WHAT KIND OF CHRISTIAN ARE YOU?

◆ ◆ ◆

1. According to the quote by S. D. Gordon, what is the Master's plan?

_____

_____

_____

_____

2. Write 2 Corinthians 3:2 in your own words. What are our lives to be?

_____

_____

_____

_____

_____

_____

_____

3. What does abiding in Christ mean, and how is this our spiritual nourishment?

_____

_____

_____

4. Where does the power to live as a Christian come from? (Read 2 Corinthians 4:7.)

_____

_____

_____

_____

5. Jesus told His disciples, *"You shall receive power when the Holy Spirit comes upon you; and you shall be witnesses to Me"* (Acts 1:8). The Greek word for power is *dunamis.* We derive the word *dynamite* from this same Greek word. What does that bring to your mind?

_____

_____

_____

_____

6. Do you see that kind of power operating in your life today?

_____

_____

_____

_____

7. What are the two reasons that we do not see more evidence of the Holy Spirit's power in the lives of individual believers today?

a. _____

_____

b. _____

_____

8. Does your current spiritual life fall into either of these categories?

_____

_____

9. Reflect upon and answer the following questions from the chapter:

a. In what ways do you abide with the Lord through His Word and prayer?

_____

_____

b. Are you seeing His power being demonstrated in your daily life?

_____

_____

c. In what ways are you experiencing victory over areas of sin and temptation in your life?

_____

_____

d. How do you experience the continual filling of the Spirit in your life?

_____

_____

e. Name some ways in which you see a deeper desire for the things of God being developed in your life.

_____

_____

_____

_____

_____

_____

_____

f. Name some ways that you are willingly yielding your life to His on a daily basis.

_____

_____

_____

_____

_____

_____

_____

g. Now spend some time with the Lord and ask Him to help you, through the transforming (*dunamis*) power of the Holy Spirit, and make you into the kind of Christian that He wants you to be.

10. What kind of Christian are you? We learned in this chapter that we will do what we want the most—what is it that you want the most in your life?

_____

_____

_____

_____

_____

_____

_____

Close your study time in prayer and ask Jesus to empower you to live more fully for Him today.

Viewing the testimony of Scripture as a whole, we cannot but concede consistent, and clear testimony to the fact that the Holy Spirit is a Divine Person, working with intelligent consciousness, infinite love and independent will. This fact and truth is of fundamental importance to Christian experience. If He is merely a power or influence, our dominant aim would be, "How may I obtain more of His power and influence?" But if He is a Divine Person, our consistent attitude should be "How can He more fully possess me so that I may become the vehicle of His power and influence?"[1]

—*J. Oswald Sanders*

WHO IS THE HOLY SPIRIT?

J. Oswald Sanders points out that a correct understanding of who the Holy Spirit is and the relationship that He desires to have with us is essential if we truly want to witness the power of God at work in our lives. As we learn about Him through the pages of Scripture, we observe His divinity—He is God. We also discover that the key to living an exciting Christian life is not found by trying to "obtain" His power for our purposes, but rather by willingly yielding our lives to His powerful influence.

A few years ago, I was asked to perform a wedding ceremony while wearing white gloves. The couple wanted to observe a cultural tradition, so I agreed. But as I was preparing for the ceremony, I began to think about how those gloves really were a good illustration of our relationship with the Holy Spirit. For instance, if I laid those gloves down on the table and commanded them to begin clapping, they would not be able to respond. If I were to ask them to move something from one place to another, they would be helpless to do so regardless of how precise I made the instructions. It is only by putting my hands inside the gloves that they have the power to do even the most basic tasks.

This is a simplistic illustration; however, it is an accurate comparison of the amount of strength that we have to live a victorious Christian life apart from the Holy Spirit. Our expectation of being able to live righteously without His indwelling Presence is equivalent to expecting an inanimate pair of gloves to be able to move about in their own strength. The Holy Spirit in our lives is like the hand inside the glove. Only through Him can we have the power to live the Christian life.

Some people today have the mistaken notion that the Holy Spirit is a "force" that can be harnessed and used for their own purposes. I always relate that mentality to the movie, Star Wars: "May the force be with you!" But the Holy Spirit is not a force, He is not an "it," and He is not a power that we can wield at our own discretion. He is a distinct Person—the third Person of the Trinity. He is God, and as such, possesses all the divine attributes of the Father and the Son.

Scripture reveals that the Holy Spirit, among other things, searches, selects, reveals, leads, teaches, comforts, guides, inspires, forbids, convicts, and reproves. He can be loved, obeyed, grieved, quenched, resisted, blasphemed, and sinned against. He is omnipotent, omniscient, and omnipresent. But nowhere in the pages of Scripture will you find even one instance where He is referred to as "it" or anything less than God Himself. Indeed, when Ananias and Sapphira tried to fool the apostle Peter in Acts chapter 5, he confronted them, saying, *"Why has Satan filled your heart to lie to the Holy Spirit? . . . You have not lied to men but to God"* (Acts 5:3–4).

Indeed, the work of the Holy Spirit is evident throughout the Bible. From the time of creation (Genesis 1:1) He has been active in the world. The Holy Spirit is also the One who inspired the writing of the Scriptures (2 Timothy 3:16). And in the Old Testament, we see how the Holy Spirit would come upon people, anointing and empowering them to accomplish specific purposes. For instance, in Exodus 31, He came upon and empowered craftsmen for the exacting task of building the tabernacle and all its furnishings. However, the Holy Spirit was not an abiding Presence during Old Testament times. He would come and go as needed, but He did not remain with them forever. In the New Testament, we see something different in the way the Holy Spirit relates to the people of God. Because of what Jesus did on the cross, the Holy Spirit is now an abiding Presence who remains with us forever.

All Christians are indwelt by the Holy Spirit at the time of salvation, and it is at that time that we are given a new nature and a new life. The Holy Spirit within the believer's heart bears witness to the fact that our lives are now His. But, each of us needs to acknowledge His Presence by yielding our wills to His in order to realize the full potential of what God desires to do in and through us. As we cooperate with the Holy Spirit, we will begin to see His plans unfolding in our lives.

THREE EXPERIENCES WITH THE HOLY SPIRIT

In John 14:17, Jesus speaks about the intimate nature of the relationship that the Holy Spirit desires to have with us. He tells the disciples, *"The world cannot receive [the Holy Spirit] . . . but you know Him."* This is very important. The Greek word that is translated "know" in this passage is *ginosko.* The predominant meaning of this word, as we see it used in this context, is to have knowledge that is grounded on personal experience. This type of knowledge is different than just having information or "head knowledge." It is experiential knowledge. In other words, it is something that you know because it has personally affected you. This difference would be similar to the difference between me saying, "I know the president," and his wife saying the same thing. I may have a lot of knowledge about the president, but she is intimately acquainted with him—she personally *knows* him. This is the kind of relationship that the Lord desires to have with each of us. God wants us to know Him intimately. He wants us to have a personal experience with Him.

Jesus further instructs His disciples in John 14:17 about their relationship to the Holy Spirit by saying that He *"dwells **with** you and will be **in** you"* (emphasis added). He is speaking to them of two separate experiences, which He differentiates here by using the words *with* and *in.* In the Greek, these two prepositions cannot always be clearly distinguished. However, in this context it is quite clear. Jesus is contrasting what they already know about the Holy Spirit (He dwells *with* you) with what they will know of Him in the future (He will be *in* you). Later, in the book of Acts, He also speaks to them of a third experience with the Holy Spirit, telling them that the Holy Spirit would come *upon* them in power. Once again, He uses a different preposition in order to denote a separate and dynamic experience that they would have one day with the Holy Spirit (He will come *upon* them in power).

Even as Christians indwelt by the Holy Spirit, our flesh still remains one of the most powerful resisting forces we will ever face.

1. He Dwells with You . . .

Until Jesus' death on the cross, the Holy Spirit had been *"with"* the disciples. That was the extent of their experience of who He was at that time. I believe that everyone has this first experience *"with"* the Holy Spirit. The Bible says the Holy Spirit is the One convicting the world of sin. He is the One who draws sinners to Christ, as He convinces them to put their trust in the Lord.

This was the experience that the disciples had with the Holy Spirit—He was drawing them to Jesus. They followed Him, they watched Him, and they finally realized who He was because the Holy Spirit was *"with"* them.

2. He Will Be in You . . .

Jesus wanted them to know that in the future the Holy Spirit was going to be *"in"* them. Up until Jesus' death and resurrection, the Holy Spirit did not dwell in the hearts of sinful people. Jesus' perfect sacrifice is what opened the way for this new work to be established. As He spoke to them in John 14:17, He was preparing them for this new, intimate relationship, which is reserved for those who are born of the Spirit. In John 3:5–8, Jesus similarly told Nicodemus:

> "Most assuredly, I say to you, unless one is born of water and the Spirit, he cannot enter the kingdom of God. That which is born of the flesh is flesh, and that which is born of the Spirit is spirit. Do not marvel that I said to you, 'You must be born again.' The wind blows where it wishes, and you hear the sound of it, but cannot tell where it comes from and where it goes. So is everyone who is born of the Spirit."

After the resurrection, the disciples received the Holy Spirit, and I believe it was at that point that they were born again (John 20:22). When we accept Jesus Christ as our Lord and Savior, we receive His life in us through the indwelling Presence of the Holy Spirit. Jesus likens the Holy Spirit's Presence in our lives to that of the wind because, like the wind, the Holy Spirit cannot be seen, but He has a powerful affect. When a person truly experiences the Lord in this way, their life will be noticeably changed. They will be more sensitive to sin and quicker to repent. They will be more interested in blessing others than in fulfilling their own needs. They will have a deeper concern for the lost than they had before. Certainly this concern for the souls of others is one of the greatest evidences that the Holy Spirit is dwelling within, because His passion for the lost becomes our passion.

When the Holy Spirit comes *"in"* us, He promises to abide with us forever. His abiding Presence in our lives signifies that His commitment to us is unconditional. If you are married, you know that it is faithfulness to the vow you made that holds your marriage together during difficult times. That commitment is the definition of true love. True love is unconditional, and it never fails because it is not based on feelings and emotions; it is based on commitment. That is the kind of love that God has toward us; it is not based on our faithfulness, but on His. And He will always remain faithful. Imagine, the Creator of the heavens and the earth loves us so much that He is willing to stoop down and dwell within the hearts of sinners such as you and me.

> *Blessed Savior, Christ most holy,*
> *In a manger Thou didst rest;*
> *Canst Thou stoop again, yet lower,*
> *And abide within my breast?*[2]
> —George Stringer Rowe

The love of God toward us is immeasurable. It far exceeds any other love that we could possibly experience. As the recipients of such a great love as this, how can we not hate the sin in our lives? How can we play around with it, and allow it to grieve the Holy Spirit and to quench His life within us? In Romans 7:18, Paul says:

> For I know that in me (that is, in my flesh) nothing
> good dwells; for to will is present with me, but how
> to perform what is good I do not find.

As Paul points out, there is a conflict within us when it comes to doing the right thing. That is because, even as Christians indwelt by the Holy Spirit, our flesh still remains one of the most powerful resisting forces we will ever face. We make choices every day. If we allow self to rule instead of the indwelling Spirit of God, we will make wrong choices and never rise above the extent of our own human limitations. We will miss the glorious heights altogether because it is only by the power that He provides through His Spirit that we are able to rise above our own sinful tendencies. And, it is only as we yield our will to His powerful influence within us that we will be able to live above the ordinary.

3. He Shall Come Upon You . . .

In Acts 1:8, Jesus addresses the issue of our powerlessness with His disciples, telling them, *"You shall receive power when the Holy Spirit has come upon you"* (emphasis added). As noted earlier, He told them this *after* they had been born again and received the Holy Spirit. So this was something different that they were going to experience in their relationship with Him—something that they had not yet known.

When the Holy Spirit comes "*upon*" us, He empowers us to be Jesus' witnesses. This is the third experience that Christians can have with the Holy Spirit; we can experience *His* power in *our* lives. This is not just for the super-spiritual; it is for every believer. A power-filled life should be the definition of what it means for us to live as Christians. But unfortunately, not every Christian would define their lives in this way because they have not experienced the Holy Spirit's power coming upon them.

Paul noticed this lack of power in the lives of some disciples that he met in Ephesus. As soon as he met them, he could sense that something was missing, so he asked them, *"Did you receive the Holy Spirit when you believed?"* (Acts 19:2). It is important to acknowledge that some scholars question whether or not these disciples were true believers. They had learned of Jesus from John the Baptist, but John was killed before the crucifixion and resurrection of the Lord took place. So, it is possible that they may not have understood the significance of all that Jesus had accomplished. But regardless of what they had or had not been taught, the point here is that their understanding of the things of Christ was incomplete. And it was visibly noticeable to Paul that what they lacked most was the power of the Holy Spirit.

This fact was confirmed by their answer to Paul's question. They said, *"We have not so much as heard whether there is a Holy Spirit"* (verse 2). At that point, Paul began instructing them more fully, teaching them all that Jesus had done, and afterward he laid hands on them and they were baptized with the Holy Spirit. At that moment, their lives were transformed as the Spirit of God came upon them in power, imparting spiritual gifts and enabling them to be His witnesses.

How would you define your Christian experience? Is His power evident in your life? If you were to encounter the apostle Paul today, do you think that he would ask you the same question that he asked the Ephesian believers? Would he say, *"Did you receive the Holy Spirit when you believed?"*

THE BAPTISM OF THE HOLY SPIRIT

Unfortunately, there is a lot of confusion and division among believers today surrounding this whole issue of being "baptized" in the Spirit. This is partly due to the many excesses and abuses that are being carried out and credited to the Holy Spirit in some circles. All the outrageous extremes, such as being slain in the Spirit, holy laughter, barking like animals, and other things that we see on Christian television are appalling. I can assure you, they have absolutely nothing to do with what the Bible teaches about the baptism of the Holy Spirit. However, because of these abuses many people are very skeptical about anything that appears too spiritual or supernatural. So, their lives are lacking in power simply because their understanding of how the Holy Spirit works is incomplete.

Part of the confusion is also due to the fact that many Christians simply do not believe in the necessity of another experience with the Holy Spirit after salvation. They feel that they received everything they needed when they accepted Jesus as their Lord and Savior. Indeed, many do receive the baptism of the Holy Spirit at the time of salvation, but it is not always the case. Jesus told His disciples to wait for the power of the Holy Spirit to come upon them after they were born again. So, while I agree that we are sealed with the Holy Spirit and receive the fullness of God at the time of salvation, I also see from Scripture that there is more that the Lord wants us to have through the baptism of the Holy Spirit.

Strange as it may seem, English Bible translators were aided in their understanding of the words used in the original biblical manuscripts to define the baptism of the Holy Spirit by an ancient recipe for making pickles. This recipe provided not only a basis for translating the archaic language, but also a great visual depiction of what happens to us when we are baptized in the Spirit. The first step in the recipe is for a cucumber to be sealed by being quickly dipped into boiling water. The word used to describe this step is *bapto*. The second step occurs when the sealed cucumber is immersed or "baptized" into a vinegar solution. The word used to describe this second process (*baptizo*) is the same word that is used to describe the "baptism" of the Holy Spirit. It is during this second process of being immersed over an extended period of time that the cucumber's characteristics are permanently changed. It becomes a pickle.

This is such a clear picture of what happens to us as Christians. Like the cucumber, first we are born again and sealed with the Holy Spirit (Ephesians 1:13). However, afterward we experience other times when the Holy Spirit comes upon us, baptizing and empowering us by His Spirit to be more Christlike in our characters. Peter's life is a good example of the kind of change that the baptism of the Holy Spirit can produce. In Acts 2, on the day of Pentecost, this man who earlier had denied the Lord and hidden in fear of the Jews, boldly proclaimed the Word of God, and three thousand people were converted in one day. What Peter was unable to do in his own strength, he was enabled to do when he was baptized in the power of the Holy Spirit.

That is what the baptism of the Holy Spirit is all about. He empowers us to live as Christ's witnesses in the world. Just as the cucumber becomes a pickle, our characters will become more like His as we are baptized in the Holy Spirit. So the question I always like to ask is: How pickled are you? Do you have the power to be His witness? Because when the Holy Spirit comes upon your life in this manner, there is a distinct difference. As a matter of fact, the greatest witness the world has of the power and love of Jesus Christ is the transforming effect that the baptism of the Holy Spirit produces in the lives of individuals.

When I was a pastoral intern, the testimony of my senior pastor, Raul Ries, was a great example to me of this transforming power of the Holy Spirit. Before he came to know the Lord, Raul was a fighter by nature. He was trained as a Marine and served during the Vietnam War. His violent nature extended to other areas of his life, including his home. He had become an abusive husband and father. His whole life was filled with rage and immorality. Then, on the day he was actually planning to kill his family, the

Holy Spirit got a hold of his heart in a very dramatic way. In the midst of his lethal rage, he turned on the television and heard the gospel as it was being preached. The convicting power of the Holy Spirit filled his heart at that very moment and changed everything.

Today Raul is a loving husband, father, and grandfather, and the pastor of a large and vibrant church. He is one of the most tender-hearted and compassionate people you will ever meet. It was the Holy Spirit who changed his life and produced in him a Christlike character that was not there before. His story is a wonderful example of what God can do when we are willing to yield our lives to His powerful influence.

Certainly, His power is something we need more of today. So, whether we choose to call it the baptism of the Holy Spirit, or the second or third experience, it really does not matter. The semantics are really not important. Look at it this way: If all you had to do in order to obtain a great treasure was to open your hand and receive it, would you do it? Of course you would. How many times? As many times as you could!

God wants to give us the greatest treasure of all in the baptism of the Holy Spirit. So, what really matters is not what we call it, but that we receive it and experience His power in our lives. So I ask you:

- Do you have the Holy Spirit?

- Do you know what gifts He has bestowed upon you?

- Are you using them?

- Is there spiritual fruit being produced in your life?

If the answer to any of these questions is no, then perhaps what is needed is the baptism of the Holy Spirit. Why not ask the Lord to pour His Spirit upon your life today?

THE HOLY SPIRIT IS GIVEN TO THOSE WHO ASK

Jesus promised the Holy Spirit to His disciples in John 14. So instead of asking *if we need to receive the Holy Sprit,* the question we should really be asking is, *how do we receive Him?* Jesus said:

> "If a son asks for bread from any father among you, will he give him a stone? Or if he asks for a fish, will he give him a serpent instead of a fish? Or if he asks for an egg, will he offer him a scorpion? If you then, being evil, know how to give good gifts to your children, how much more will your heavenly Father give the Holy Spirit to those who ask Him!"

—LUKE 11:11–13

A lot of Christians simply do not ask the Father for the Holy Spirit. That is why a good number of believers who possess eternal life are devoid of the power to live for Christ, because they simply do not ask.

A. W. Tozer once said, *"You can have as much of God as you want."*[3] The Lord wants us to ask for and receive everything that the Holy Spirit has for us. Yet, either because our understanding is darkened or because our hands are filled with the trinkets of this world, we do not ask. It is as though the Lord wants to give us a sumptuous filet mignon dinner, but we choose to keep on eating dog food.

It is the responsibility of every believer to ask for the Holy Spirit. Without the Holy Spirit, we will not have the power to be witnesses of Christ or to:

- Boldly speak His Word.
- Be victorious over bad habits and attitudes that have enslaved us.
- Say no to things that are wrong.
- Choose to be inconvenienced rather than to act selfishly.
- Admit our shortcomings, failures, and sins.
- Forgive, and ask for others' forgiveness.
- Understand and obey the Word of God.
- Pray and care for those in need.

- Love people (even the unlovable ones).

- Encourage instead of criticize.

- Take responsibility for our actions (even when it is costly to do so).

- Follow Him no matter where He leads.

- Demonstrate spiritual gifts and bear spiritual fruit in our lives.

By cultivating a habit of continually asking for and yielding to the Spirit of God, we make ourselves available for His purposes. Yielding to the Holy Spirit, therefore, positions us to be used by God at any given time. This is why a yielded life is a powerful one, because it is available for God. It has been said, *"It is not how much of God that I have, but how much of me that He has."* That is what really matters. When you wake up in the morning, the prayer of your heart should be, *"Lord, cleanse me and fill me, help me and empower me in this day."*

Over one hundred years ago, two young men were talking in Ireland. One said, *"The world has yet to see what God will do with a man who is fully consecrated to Him."* The other man meditated on that thought for weeks. It so gripped him that one day he exclaimed, *"By the Holy Spirit in me I'll be that man."* Historians now say that he touched two continents for Christ. His name was Dwight L. Moody.[4]

How about you? What are you asking the Lord for today? Are you settling for dog food? Or are you asking Him for the Holy Spirit—for the power to put down sin and live a life consecrated to the Lord? D. L. Moody said, *"It lies with each man himself whether he will or will not make that entire and full consecration."*[5] He was just one man, but he was a man who took the Lord at His Word. Imagine what the world would be like if Christians everywhere took God at His Word.

Imagine what your life would be like if you took God at His Word. Jesus said if we ask for the Holy Spirit, He would be given to us. Imagine the difference we could make in our world today if we all lived as D. L. Moody did one hundred years ago.

In his letter to the Ephesians, Paul prayed that they would experience the fullness of God. It is also my prayer for us today.

> For this reason I bow my knees to the Father of our Lord Jesus Christ, from whom the whole family in heaven and earth is named, that He would grant you, according to the riches of His glory, to be strengthened with might through His Spirit in the inner man, that Christ may dwell in your hearts through faith; that you, being rooted and grounded in love, may be able to comprehend with all the saints what is the width and length and depth and height—to know the love of Christ which passes knowledge; that you may be filled with all the fullness of God.
>
> —EPHESIANS 3:14–19

Chapter Two Study Guide

WHO IS THE HOLY SPIRIT?

♦ ♦ ♦

1. What do the Scriptures reveal to us about nature of the Holy Spirit?

_____

_____

2. What are the three experiences a believer can have with the Holy Spirit? Briefly explain the differences between each one.

a. _____

_____

b. _____

_____

c. _____

_____

3. The Scriptures say that the Holy Spirit is like the wind. Explain how that analogy can be applied in a life that is filled with the Spirit.

_____

_____

4. What is one of the greatest evidences that the Holy Spirit is dwelling within a believer?

_____

_____

5. How does the difference between the Greek words *bapto* and *baptizo* help us to understand what being baptized in the Holy Spirit means?

_____

_____

6. According to Luke 11:11–13, how do Christians get the Holy Spirit?

_____

_____

7. Do you have the Holy Spirit? Are you experiencing His transforming power in your life?

_____

_____

8. Name some practical ways that you need the power of the Holy Spirit in your daily life.

_____

_____

9. Did you know that the Holy Spirit will help you to:

- Boldly speak His Word

- Be victorious over bad habits and attitudes that have enslaved you

- Say no to things that are wrong

- Admit your shortcomings, failures, and sins

- Forgive, and ask for others' forgiveness

- Understand and obey the Word of God

- Pray and care for those in need
- Love the unlovable
- Encourage instead of criticize
- Take responsibility for your actions
- Follow Him no matter where He leads
- Demonstrate spiritual gifts and bear spiritual fruit in your life

a. Does it surprise you that the Holy Spirit can help you in these areas?

_____

_____

_____

_____

b. In what area of your life right now is the Lord showing you that you need His power?

_____

_____

_____

_____

In his letter to the Ephesians, Paul prayed that they would continue to experience the fullness of God. Read Ephesians 3:14–19 below and fill in the blanks with your name to make these Scriptures a personal prayer between you and the Lord.

> For this reason I bow my knees to the Father of our
> Lord Jesus Christ, from whom the whole family in
> heaven and earth is named, that He would grant

_____, according to the riches of His glory, to be strengthened with might through His Spirit in the inner man, that Christ may dwell in _____ heart through faith, that _____, being rooted and grounded in love, may be able to comprehend with all the saints what is the width and length and depth and height— to know the love of Christ which passes knowledge; that _____ may be filled with all the fullness of God.

Ask the Lord to answer this prayer in your life so that you can walk in the fullness of God each day.

As long as your flesh is indulged and suffered to remain, there is no way for you to enter into the Holiest of all. You cannot see it. The old nature hinders your seeing the glory of God. But when self dies, the veil is torn in two, the glory of God is revealed, and the voice of the Spirit says: "Having therefore . . . boldness to enter into the holiest by the blood of Jesus, by a new and living way, which he hath consecrated for us, through the veil, that is to say his flesh . . . let us draw near with a true heart in full assurance of faith" (Hebrews 10:19–20, 22 [KJV]).

Everything, therefore, that helps you to die to self helps you to live in Him and is the opening up of the glory of God to you. If you can say, "I am dead with Christ," and, "I am risen with Christ," you can understand something of the apostle's language when he prays "that Christ may dwell in your hearts by faith; that ye . . . may be able to comprehend . . . the breadth, and length, and depth, and height; and to know the love of Christ, which passeth knowledge, that ye might be filled with all the fullness of God" (Ephesians 3:17–19 [KJV]).

Has the veil been rent in twain for you by the death of self? If so, your heart is a holy Tabernacle, and there is no barrier between you and the throne of God.[1]

—*A. B. Simpson*

PREPARING A PLACE FOR THE LORD

It has been said that within the heart of every man there is a God-shaped vacuum, a void that can only be filled by God Himself. Perhaps we were created this way so that we would always have a sense of God's rightful place in our lives.

In the Old Testament, God's rightful place among His people was in the tabernacle, and later in the temple in Jerusalem. One of the greatest truths revealed in the New Testament is that the Holy Spirit now dwells within the heart of every believer (2 Corinthians 1:22). Today our hearts are His holy tabernacle—His dwelling place. And when we willingly yield to His Presence within, it will spark a revolution in our lives. Andrew Murray said,

> True revival means nothing less than a revolution, casting out the spirit of worldliness and selfishness and making God and His love triumph in the heart and life.[2]

However, in order for such a work of revival to take place in our lives, the Holy Spirit needs to be more than just a guest; He needs to be master over all.

His Presence in our lives is the reason the condition of our hearts is so important to the Lord. His Word is full of clear exhortation with regard to this subject. For instance, Proverbs 4:23 cautions us, *"Keep your heart with all diligence, for out of it spring the issues of life."* Jesus also spoke about the importance of tending our hearts when He said, *"Out of the abundance of the heart the mouth speaks"* (Matthew 12:34). And in case we have any doubt as to the natural state of our hearts, the prophet Jeremiah gave us a very clear assessment of man's "spiritual heart condition" when he said, *"The heart is deceitful above all things, and desperately wicked; who can know it?"* (Jeremiah 17:9). It is certainly true, what comes out of our lives (in the things that we do and say) is a direct result of that which is ruling in our hearts!

Obviously when the Bible refers to the heart, it is not speaking about the physical organ that pumps blood through our veins. Our heart is the center of our life, the seat of our will and emotions, the place within us that drives the outer life. Scripture attributes our understanding, thoughts, emotions, judgments, motives, desires, and affections to the heart. Indeed, all the issues of life do spring from one place: the heart. And it is in that strategic place in our lives that the Spirit of God takes up residence.

Ephesians 3:17 says that Christ *"dwell[s] in your hearts through faith."* The word *dwell* suggests the idea of "settling in." When we receive Jesus Christ as our Savior, the Holy Spirit enters into the very center of our lives, making our hearts His home. A. B. Simpson once wrote a stanza that captures this awesome truth:

> *This is my wonderful story,*
> *Christ to my heart has come;*
> *Jesus, the King of Glory,*
> *Finds in my heart a home.*[3]

THE DWELLING PLACE OF THE LORD

In the book of 1 Kings, we have an account of the building and dedication of the first temple in Jerusalem by King Solomon. When the priests brought the ark and all the holy furnishings into the temple, the awesome Presence of God came and rested on that place. *"The glory of the LORD filled the house of the LORD"* (1 Kings 8:11). His holy Presence occupied every inch of space within, leaving room for nothing else. The people had to stand outside in awe, praising and worshiping the Lord.

What a day that must have been when the Spirit of God was present among His people in all His glory. But unfortunately, not too long afterward, the nation of Israel allowed the temple of the Lord to fall into disrepair. They had forgotten His glory and neglected the care of His home. They disregarded the relationship they had with Him. In fact, until the days of King Hezekiah, they lived with indifference to His holiness (2 Chronicles 29–32). However, when Hezekiah inherited the throne, he immediately went to work making the temple a fit place for the Spirit of God to dwell in once again. From his example, we can glean some very practical lessons on preparing and keeping our hearts as temples fit for His Presence.

Opening the Door

The first thing Hezekiah did was to open and repair the temple doors so that the people could have access to God's Presence (2 Chronicles 29:3). Access to God is the first step we need to take in our relationship to the Lord as well. That is because sin alienated us from God, but when Jesus died on the cross He took care of the sin that separated us. At the very moment of His death, the veil in the temple, which separated the people from the Presence of God, was torn in two from top to bottom (Matthew 27:51). No human hand could have done that; it was the hand of God, and it symbolized how Jesus' death on the cross opened the door for us to have fellowship with the Lord once again.

When we trust in Jesus for our salvation, we receive access to God and we are sealed with the Holy Spirit.

> In Him you also trusted, after you heard the word of truth, the gospel of your salvation; in whom also, having believed, you were sealed with the Holy Spirit of promise, who is the guarantee of our inheritance until the redemption of the purchased possession, to the praise of His glory.
>
> —Ephesians 1:13–14

The old temple in Jerusalem is no longer needed. Everything that it symbolized—the altars and the sacrifices, the holy implements, the oil, and the incense—were all a foreshadowing of that which was fulfilled in Jesus Christ, the Messiah.

H is glory is hindered by only one thing—the amount of room that we allow Him to occupy.

Today, through the Person of the Holy Spirit, the same awesome glory that rested upon the temple in Jerusalem dwells within the heart of every born-again believer. It has been said that His glory is hindered by only one thing—the amount of room that we allow Him to occupy. Just like on the day when King Solomon dedicated the temple, His glorious Presence can fill every inch of His new home. However, unless we yield the control of each area of our lives to Him, we will not enjoy the fullness of His glorious Presence.

It is my confident belief that there is not a single man or woman who believes in Christ who has not Christ in the heart. But remember, that as the heavy veil hid the holy of holies from the holy place, so Jesus Christ may be in your heart; but because you have never recognized that He is there, because you have no use of His presence there, because you have been unbelieving, and maybe indolent to respond to His appeal, though He has been in your heart ever since you were regenerate, His presence has been hidden from your eyes; it has been veiled. I pray God that the two hands that rent the veil of the temple in twain from the top to the bottom, may rend the veil in your inner life that the Christ who is there may be revealed in you.[4]

—F. B. Meyer

Try to picture your heart as the Lord's temple. Has that veil of separation been rent in two by the Savior's own hand? Are others drawn to the warm glow from the light of His love as it shines brightly within? Does the sweet aroma of the incense of prayer permeate the air as it rises, unhindered, into His holy Presence? Are you satisfying your hungry soul with the fresh Bread of Life that He prepares for you each day? Or have you neglected His home? Is yours a temple in need of repair? Has the light grown dim within? Have you neglected the house of the Lord?

CLEANING HOUSE

Once the doors to the temple had been opened and repaired, the next thing that Hezekiah did was to go in and clean out the house of God (2 Chronicles 4–19). Over the years of neglect, all kinds of rubbish had accumulated within. In its current condition, the temple was an abomination to the Lord and completely useless for the holy purposes for which God had intended. The doors were open, but because the people had neglected the things of God, His dwelling place had become defiled and their fellowship was hindered.

Neglect occurs when we simply do nothing long enough. Our garages are usually a good example of the effects of neglect and the problems it can cause. Usually, it is not until we are hopelessly overwhelmed by the clutter, and unable to find anything anymore, that we realize the consequences of our inaction.

Spiritually speaking, doing nothing can lead to such problems as well, and that is exactly what the nation of Israel discovered. The lesson that we learn from Hezekiah at this point is the necessity of bringing everything that is concealed into the light. He instructed the priests to go into the inner part of the house of the Lord and to carry out all the rubbish from within. It took them eight days just to bring it all into the light of the outer courtyard.

Maybe that is what some of us are in need of today—a good "temple" cleaning—a cleansing of our hearts, a transforming and powerful inner work of the Lord in our lives. Just as Hezekiah sent the priests in to clean out the house of the Lord, Jesus has sent the Holy Spirit into the center of our lives. As we yield to Him, He will sweep out every dark corner, and our lives will become set apart for the purposes that God has intended.

Is there any clutter in your heart today? Remember, it is Christ's home and He is there to help you sort through the mess. Maybe you have a physical dependency on alcohol, drugs, pornography, or something else that has gotten a hold of your life. You think it is harmless and nobody knows, but that is not true. Remember, your heart is Christ's home. He knows what is hidden in those dark corners, and His Word says, *"Be sure your sin will find you out"* (Numbers 32:23).

For others, the clutter might be an illicit relationship, or even a friendship with someone of the opposite sex that has gone too far. How do you know if it has gone further than it should have? If a picture of that person just flashed through your mind, you'd better be careful because that relationship has probably gone too far.

Maybe your life has become cluttered with more "acceptable" sins, such as pride, arrogance, or self-righteousness. You can mask these pretty well sometimes, but the Lord knows the motives of your heart; nothing escapes His notice.

Perhaps anger, bitterness, resentment, or an unforgiving attitude have crept in to defile His dwelling place. These are probably the most deadly sins of all because they wrap themselves so tightly around your heart that you do not see them, and worse yet, they will cause you to forsake the Lord's mercy in your life.

Greed and covetousness also tend to creep in unnoticed, but before long, the riches of this world can cause you to lose sight of the greatest treasure of all. That is why Jesus said, *"Where your treasure is, there your heart will be also"* (Matthew 6:21).

Yes, just like in our garages, a whole lot of junk can accumulate in our hearts without much effort at all, simply because we tend to neglect painful issues and wrong motives. We are comfortable as long as nothing is disturbed, but what we really need to do is the same thing that Hezekiah did—we need to clean house. Remember, the Holy Spirit is within you and He is present to take out all the trash that is cluttering up His home. Oh, that we would be willing to let Him have His rightful place in the center of our lives.

A New Life Within

Most of us need to be challenged, periodically, in our Christian walk. We need to evaluate whose life is really in control. The questions we must ask ourselves are these:

1. What is on my heart?

2. What is on my lips?

3. What is on my mind?

4. What is on display in my life?

By honestly answering these four questions we will be able to see those areas in our lives that are not fully under the control of the Holy Spirit.

1. What is on my heart?

Our hearts are now the Lord's home. So, if Jesus is in our hearts, then He will be the greatest passion of our lives. Is He? Can you truly say that the deepest longing of your life today is to be in His Presence? Do you agree with King David in Psalm 27:4 when he said that the *one* thing he desired was to be with the Lord? Or has something else taken hold of your heart? If you are not sure of the answer to this question, try this exercise. Draw a circle. That circle represents your life. Write down whatever is pressing most on your heart today in the middle of that circle. That is what your life is revolving around! Is it Jesus? Or has something else taken His place? When anything, whether good or bad, takes His place in our lives, it is idolatry.

How about others? Do you have a heart for the lost and an awareness of the need that is all around you, in your family, on the job, and in your neighborhood? Do you desire for God to give you opportunities everywhere you go to share His love, both in word and deed, with those who do not know Him? This is not to say that we should become pushy and obnoxious Christians, getting in everyone's face about the Lord, whether they want to hear it or not. That would not be a true reflection of the life of Christ. Rather, when His life is ruling in our hearts, we will have a genuine concern for the welfare of others, so much so that we will want to live in such a way that they will see Jesus in all we do and say. This is what our lives in Christ are all about—He lights a holy fire of love within us that longs to bring others into His Presence.

2. What is on my lips?

In Luke 19:46, Jesus said, *"My house is a house of prayer."* So, if His home is now in our hearts, then it would make sense that Jesus would desire for our lives to be filled with prayer. I believe much of the weakness and ineffectiveness that we see in the body of Christ today is directly related to a lack of waiting on the Lord in prayer. Prayer is an expression of our dependency upon God. It is the most necessary and important occupation of every Christian. Prayer ought to be our greatest joy, our greatest privilege, our greatest work, and our greatest priority. If He is ruling in our hearts, then prayer will be found on our lips. So, how is your prayer life?

Oftentimes many of us find it is easier to work than to pray. That is because we would rather operate in our strengths than in our weaknesses. Prayer is a weakness. We simply do not know how to pray, but God has provided the Holy Spirit to help us.

> The Spirit also helps in our weaknesses. For we do not know what we should pray for as we ought, but the Spirit Himself makes intercession for us with groanings which cannot be uttered. Now He who searches the hearts knows what the mind of the

Spirit is, because He makes intercession for the saints according to the will of God.

—ROMANS 8:26–27

We cannot pray according to the will of God without His help. Jesus said, *"Without Me you can do nothing"* (John 15:5). So, our prayer lives will benefit when we learn what the apostle Paul knew about relying on Jesus, *"I can do all things through Christ who strengthens me"* (Philippians 4:13). A person of power is undoubtedly a person of prayer. As we yield to the Holy Spirit, He will strengthen us and fill our lives with words of prayer.

3. What is on my mind?

If Jesus has made it possible for the Holy Spirit to dwell in my heart, then His grace should be what is on my mind. What we think about our relationship with God is very important. Sometimes we can have a "works" mentality, thinking that we can earn God's favor. This creeps into our lives more often than we realize. We know we are saved by grace, but we can live differently. As a result, we can become competitive with one another and legalistic in our walks with the Lord. We can begin imposing our standards of holiness onto the lives of others and totally miss the work of His grace. However, whether we are at our worst, or at our best, His love for us remains the same because it is in Christ alone that we are made worthy of heaven.

If I got the opportunity to go to the White House and speak to the president, I would be in his presence solely because of what he did in inviting me in. Without an invitation, nothing I did to get there would matter. Even if I were the best citizen in the land, I would not get past the guard. Similarly, we all come into the Lord's Presence because of Jesus' righteousness, not our own. That truth is our assurance. When we stray from it, we will experience an up and down walk with the Lord. None of us is worthy to stand in His Presence (we all fall short); however, through Jesus it has been made possible. Our works, no matter how good they may be, can never meet the standard of holiness that God sets before us. It is only in Christ that we have the *"hope of glory"* (Colossians 1:27). He is our salvation. He is our invitation. As we yield to the Holy Spirit, He will constantly bring our minds back to Jesus.

4. What is on display in my life?

- Is your life a demonstration of the power of God?

- Is He on display for others to see?

- Are you overcoming sin?

- Are you growing in the Lord?

If Jesus is at home in our hearts, then His life will be seen in us. Jesus said that we are to live in such a way that those around us would give glory to our Father in heaven. Unfortunately, this is not always the case. While it is true that most Christians come to the Lord because they are influenced by the life of another believer, it is also true that many people reject Christianity because of what they see in the lives of some Christians. In 1 Corinthians 3:1–3, Paul helps us to understand this divergence by identifying the problem. He points out the fact that Christians can live one of two ways. We can be spiritual, or we can be carnal:

> And I, brethren, could not speak to you as to *spiritual* people but as to *carnal*, as to babes in Christ. I fed you with milk and not with solid food; for until now you were not able to receive it, and even now you are still not able; for you are still carnal. For where there are envy, strife, and divisions among you, are you not carnal and behaving like mere men? (emphasis added)

Paul was exhorting the Corinthian believers, because by this time they should have been exhibiting a level of spiritual maturity in their Christian lives, but it was not evident. *Carnal* means "flesh." The ruling force in the lives of the Corinthian believers was still their fleshly desires and lusts. This had stunted their spiritual growth. Later on, Paul rebuked them once again for their carnal lifestyle, saying:

> Do you not know that your body is the temple of the Holy Spirit who is in you, whom you have from God, and you are not your own?
>
> —1 CORINTHIANS 6:19

The Corinthians needed to be reminded of their holy purpose, and so do we. Our lives are no longer our own—we belong to Christ. When we allow the flesh to rule, the life of Christ will not be seen in us, but when we are yielded to the Holy Spirit, He will lift up the name of Jesus in our lives for all to see.

THE FLESH AND THE SPIRIT

In his book, *The Holy Spirit*, Billy Graham illustrates the battle that exists between the flesh and the Spirit, and the secret of being victorious every time:

> An Eskimo fisherman came to town every Saturday afternoon. He always brought his two dogs with him. One was white and the other was black. He had taught them to fight on command. Every Saturday afternoon in the town square these two dogs would fight and the fishermen would take bets [on which dog would win]. On one Saturday the black dog would win; another Saturday, the white dog would win—but the fisherman always won! His friends began to ask him how he did it. [They wanted to know the secret of his accuracy.] He said, "I starve one and feed the other. The one I feed always wins because he is stronger."[5]

It is like that spiritually too. Whichever "dog" we feed will win. Each time we yield to our fleshly desires, we are feeding the old carnal nature, and it will grow stronger. Likewise, if we yield to the things of the Spirit, then we will grow stronger spiritually, and the desires of the flesh will not so easily overcome us. In Galatians, Paul tells us exactly what the works of the flesh are.

> The works of the flesh are evident, which are: adultery, fornication, uncleanness, lewdness, idolatry, sorcery, hatred, contentions, jealousies, outbursts of wrath, selfish ambitions, dissensions, heresies, envy, murders, drunkenness, revelries, and the like . . .
>
> —GALATIANS 5:19–21

As we yield our hearts to the Spirit, these things will not control us. It really is that simple. God has done His part; now we must do ours. He has made the "spiritual deposit" into our accounts; it is now up to us to "write the checks." We must choose to avail ourselves of His Spirit by allowing Him to rule our hearts. As we do so, His Presence is manifest and can be seen in our lives through the fruits and gifts of the Spirit.

- The fruit of the Spirit is love, joy, peace, longsuffering, kindness, goodness, faithfulness, gentleness, self-control (Galatians 5:22–23).

- The gifts of the Spirit include: words of wisdom, words of knowledge, faith, gifts of healings, working of miracles, prophecy, discerning of spirits, different kinds of tongues, interpretation of tongues, ministering, teaching, exhortation, giving, leading, and mercy (1 Corinthians 12:7–10; Romans 12:6–8).

We are heirs to the glorious promises of eternity in Christ. The Holy Spirit within is our down payment; He is our promissory note. He is our guarantee that we will one day receive the full payment of our salvation, which is the redemption of our physical bodies. However, until then we still have our old sinful natures to contend with, but the difference is that through the indwelling Presence of the Holy Spirit, we have now received a new nature (His nature) and a new heart (His heart). *"If anyone is in Christ, he is a new creation"* (2 Corinthians 5:17). So, we now have a choice that we did not have before. We can choose whether or not we will yield ourselves to the old nature of the flesh or to the new nature of the Spirit.

> Walk in the Spirit, and you shall not fulfill the lust of the flesh. For the flesh lusts against the Spirit, and the Spirit against the flesh; and these are contrary to one another.
> —GALATIANS 5:16–17

BEND US O LORD

At the turn of the century, a preacher closed a prayer meeting in Wales with these simple words, *"Bend us O Lord."* (*Bend*, in Welsh, means "to be entirely submitted to.") A man by the name of Evan Roberts was so moved by these words that he cried out, *"Bend me O God. Bend me!"* When asked later what had "bent" him, he said, *"I saw for the first time that Jesus died for ME—He bent me with His love."*

He finally understood the depth of his sin that night, and the glorious provision that Christ had made for him. He willingly yielded himself to live under His influence. Later, he offered this advice to those who desire to experience this kind of personal revival in their own lives:

> The Holy Spirit within is our down payment; He is our promissory note.

1. Confess any known sin.
   [Be honest—stop hiding, covering up, and excusing your sin. Bring it out into the light.]

2. Put away any doubtful habit.
   [Give up anything that you have to keep convincing yourself is okay.]

3. Obey the Spirit promptly.
   [Do not let doubts or fears get in the way of obedience.]

4. Confess Christ openly.
   [Stop trying to fit into the world's mold—be honest about who you are and who you believe in.] [6]

It has been said, *"Christ is not sweet until sin is made bitter."* In other words, in order to really appreciate Christ's sacrifice and fully experience His Presence in our lives, we need to acknowledge the depth of sin within our own hearts. If we compare ourselves with others, instead of with Jesus, we may think we are doing okay, when in reality we are not. If we miss the depths of our own need, we will also miss the incredible resources available to us in Christ. We will never truly know the vastness of His provision until we recognize the plague within our own hearts.

An unknown Christian author wrote the following thoughts around AD 1100. They are a timeless illustration of how change always begins in our own hearts. He wrote:

> When I was a young man, I wanted to change the world. I found it was difficult to change the world, so I tried to change my nation. When I found I couldn't change the nation, I began to focus on my town. I couldn't change the town and as an older man, I tried to change my family. Now, as an old man, I realize the only thing I can change is myself, and suddenly I realize that if long ago I had changed myself, I could have made an impact on my family. My family and I could

have made an impact on our town. Their impact could have changed the nation and I could indeed have changed the world.

Through the Holy Spirit, we have been given a whole new capacity for life. But it is only when we willingly allow Him to have full dominion in our hearts that we will be able to experience for ourselves the sweetness of His Presence.

We should ask the Lord to do a fresh work in our hearts on a regular basis so that our lives are a demonstration of the power of the Holy Spirit. We need to put away those idols and ask Him to keep the fires within stoked and burning red hot. We need to let Jesus empty out the trash so that the Holy Spirit can fill every inch of His new home.

Chapter Three Study Guide

PREPARING A PLACE FOR THE LORD

◆　◆　◆

1. Write out 2 Corinthians 1:22 below.

_____

_____

_____

_____

   a. Where does the Holy Spirit dwell?

_____

_____

_____

   b. Why do you think it is critical for Him to settle there?

_____

_____

_____

2. Drawing on the example given in 2 Chronicles 29–32, what two things did Hezekiah do to make the temple a proper place for the Spirit of God to dwell?

   a. _____

_____

   b. _____

_____

3. Can you draw a parallel to your own heart: What things are cluttering up your life today?

_____

_____

_____

4. What four areas are key to assessing whether or not we are living our lives under the influence of the Holy Spirit? Briefly explain each one.

   a. _____

   _____

   b. _____

   _____

   c. _____

   _____

   d. _____

   _____

5. From the previous question, name which area in your life needs to be more yielded to the Holy Spirit's influence.

_____

_____

_____

6. From the story about the two dogs, what is the secret to being victorious in walking in the Spirit?

_____

_____

7. Reflect on your answer to the last question. Which "dog" are you feeding the most and what are you feeding it?

_____

_____

8. Write the four instructions listed by Evan Roberts to those who desire to experience a personal revival. As you write each one, take time to apply them personally to your own spiritual life.

a. _____

_____

b. _____

_____

c. _____

_____

d. _____

_____

9. Have you asked the Lord to take up residence in your heart? What changes have you noticed since?

_____

_____

_____

10. Have you given Him permission to change you by doing whatever is necessary in your life?

_____

_____

_____

11. Do you desire that the Holy Spirit would revive you today?

_____

_____

Resolve to make a fresh commitment to the Lord and let Him know that you desire a personal revival in your heart. Tell Him that you want Him to have His way in your life and then relinquish anything that has taken His place.

Has the Spirit of God been searching your heart and convicting you of lack of grace, of love, of gentleness, of Christ-likeness? Have you seen yourself as lacking in reality and joy, with no true evidence of His life in you? Does your heart cry out today for His cleansing as you confess before Him with a humble and broken spirit? Then to you I say, claim your anointing today, for God has promised that the fire of His Spirit and the glowing reality of His love will always descend upon that yielded life which places no confidence in the flesh but hungers for a God-renewed heart of holiness and righteousness. The recognition of heaven is the mark of your election, to all the world the revelation that you belong to Jesus. Is this anointing on you today? Is there the mark of reality in your spiritual life?[1]

—*Alan Redpath*

THE MARK OF A YIELDED LIFE

Someone once asked the question: *"If your Christianity was on trial today, would there be enough evidence to convict you?"* There should be! You and I have absolutely no excuse for living nominal Christian lives any longer. The indwelling Spirit of God is present to help and guide us, comfort and empower us; He will transform our lives and make us more like Jesus. Indeed, the Holy Spirit:

- Empowers us (by imparting His life to us)

- Sanctifies us (by setting us apart for His purposes)

- Transforms us (by changing our character from the inside out)

So, as we yield to His powerful influence, evidence of His Presence in our lives will abound. Just as I can prove that I live in my house because my name is on the deed, my clothes are in the closet, and my favorite food is in the refrigerator, so too, if He is at home in my heart, proof will be found.

The Holy Spirit is an influence for good on all we think, do, and say. As we yield to Him, our decisions, attitudes, behavior, and speech will all reflect the reality of Christ's life within. The question is: Are we availing ourselves of His Presence?

Truthfully, we can no longer say that we cannot live the Christian life, but only that we will not choose to do so. We must willingly choose to live under His authority. That is why some Christians grow in leaps and bounds, while others can be saved for twenty years with very little evidence of His Presence in their lives. They have not grown simply because they have not yielded their will to His. Therefore, knowing what the Holy Spirit can do in our lives is only half the equation. The other half is actually being able to tell if we are filled with the Spirit at any given moment. So how can we know whether or not we are filled with the Spirit?

Being filled with the Spirit is the only way to live continually under His influence.

CONTRASTING INFLUENCES

In Ephesians 5:18, the apostle Paul writes, *"Do not be drunk with wine, in which is dissipation; but be filled with the Spirit."* We have no reason to believe that alcoholism was a problem that Paul needed to address with the church of Ephesus. Rather, he uses an ageless illustration in order to teach an important lesson. Being filled with the Spirit is the only way to live continually under His influence. By contrasting the negative influence that alcohol can have on our lives with that of the Spirit-filled life, Paul is making a distinction between the world's influence and that of the Holy Spirit. He is, in effect, saying, *"Hey, don't settle for being under the dissipating influence of alcohol when you can choose to be filled with the life-giving Spirit of God."*

Indeed, there are both similarities and differences between being drunk (under the influence of ethyl alcohol) and being under the influence of the Holy Spirit. For instance, alcohol has a controlling effect on those who choose to be under its influence. People enjoy drinking at first because it gives them a feeling of euphoria and freedom. It helps them to feel less inhibited and more confident, friendly, and gregarious—they are the life of the party. It distracts them from all their problems and worries; they can forget about themselves for a little while. But the carefree feelings that alcohol can produce are very deceiving. The initial effect on a person's life may be stimulating and energizing, but in reality, alcohol is a drug that is actually depressing the higher functions of the user's brain. It impairs the senses, blocking out balance, judgment, and reason. And although at first people may feel liberated, in the end its addicting qualities will only serve to bring them into greater bondage. People who allow alcohol to govern them will eventually lose control of their lives.

Paul calls this *dissipation*, or "wasteful living." People tend to squander valuable resources when they are in alcohol's grip. Instead of building up their lives, alcohol's influence, over time, tears them down. Those under its control will make promises that they fail to keep, and even worse, they will disregard their purity, health, safety, and innocence. That is because alcohol inhibits their ability to make good judgments, so they act foolishly even though they think they are being reasonable and responsible. Alcohol is a great deceiver, and it will destroy every good thing in a person's life when he or she yields to its influence.

Christianity is not defined by what we abstain from; it is defined by the One whose life we embrace.

Unfortunately, there are many who view Christianity through the eyes of deception as well. Much of the culture today thinks that the moral standards held by the church are too restrictive and are intended to take all the fun out of life. However, true Christianity is not defined by what we abstain from; it is defined by the One whose life we embrace. What the world cannot understand is that life in the Spirit is truly an invigorating life because it is Christ's life in us. His Spirit sustains us and directs us as we yield to Him. I once heard a message by Vance Havner in which he said, *"There is only one Christian life that has ever been lived, and He [Jesus] wants to live it in you."*

Unlike the effects of alcohol, when a person is fully yielded to the Holy Spirit—who knows all things—He will come alongside and expand his or her ability to reason and to make good judgments. Under His influence, a person will also experience real power and transformation. Relationships will improve, and there will now be victory over the sin and temptation that has hindered them in the past. A person under the influence of the Spirit will be faithful in word and in deed. And, in contrast to the dissipation that occurs in the life of someone who is given over to the influence of alcohol, a life lived under the influence of the Holy Spirit is never wasted.

Life under the influence of the Holy Spirit is the only choice we can make that will continually set us free from the tyranny of our flesh.

In addition, when we are yielded to the influence of the Holy Spirit, He gives us the strength we need to go through whatever difficulty we may be facing. Unlike alcohol, which will only serve to help us temporarily forget our troubles, the Holy Spirit teaches and reminds us along the way that there is purpose connected with everything in our lives, and that God makes *"all things work together for good to those who love [Him], to those who are the called according to His purpose"* (Romans 8:28).

So, while some may think that Christianity is a stifling road that is just too hard to travel, in reality it is actually the way of greater freedom. Life under the influence of the Holy Spirit is the only choice we can make that will continually set us free from the tyranny of our flesh.

Paul uses this contrast to show the better path that God desires for us. The questions that we all need to ask and answer are: What am I yielding my life to today? Am I yielded to the Spirit? Or, have I given myself over to the control of some other influence? And, lest you think you are okay just because you are not an alcoholic or a drug addict, I want you to understand something: If you are not living a Spirit-filled life, you too are wasting the resources, the opportunities, and the time that God has given you. Remember, Paul not only said that we *are not* to be drunk, but also that we *are* to *"be filled with the Spirit"!* How do we do this? How do we know if we are filled with the Holy Spirit?

STAYING FILLED

If we want to be continually filled with the Holy Spirit, the first thing we need to understand is the gentle and gracious way in which the Lord deals with us. He will never override our free will. It is always our choice to yield to Him, and only as we choose to do so will we experience the fullness of His Spirit. It seems like it would be easier if God would just prevent us from making poor decisions (it would save us a lot of pain too), but life in the Spirit is a choice we willingly make when we submit our lives to His leading.

The second thing we need to understand is that He will give us all the power we need to live for Him. As noted earlier, the Spirit-filled life does not consist of a set of moral laws, as some have believed. The law is just a mirror, and a mirror only reveals things; it cannot change anything. However, life in the Spirit is His life ruling in our hearts; and that changes everything. Understanding this distinction—between depending upon our own abilities and trusting in His—is an important aspect in staying filled with the Spirit. We need to cease from all our own efforts of trying to live the Christian life and cooperate fully with what the Lord is doing in us.

Living under the influence of the Holy Spirit, therefore, is remarkably simple, though radically different, from the way the world lives. Living under His influence is continually choosing to rely on God's ability instead of our own. What God began in our lives, He will complete as we yield to and cooperate with His ongoing purposes.

Finally, we need to recognize those things in our lives that are hindering us from being filled with the Spirit. For instance, Scripture warns us not to:

1. Grieve the Holy Spirit (Ephesians 4:30)

The word *grieve* is used here to describe God's heart toward us in human terms. In this way, we get a sense of how sin affects our relationship with Him. When we allow our flesh to be the dominant influence (giving way to lusts, passions, and desires), then His love and power can no longer be fully expressed through us. That "grieves" the heart of God.

2. Quench the Spirit (1 Thessalonians 5:19)

To *quench* means "to extinguish," "to put out the flame." We quench the Holy Spirit's life in us when we disobey and resist His leading. If we want His life to continually flow through ours, then we need to obey the Spirit promptly. We need to immediately confess and repent of any sin that He reveals to us instead of making excuses for our behavior.

3. Ignore His Presence (John 14:16–18)

If we want to be filled with the Spirit on a continual basis, then we need to acknowledge His Presence. Jesus said that He would not leave us as orphans. He said that He would send the Holy Spirit to help us. We need to pay attention to the way the Holy Spirit wants to work in our lives, and make ourselves available to Him.

4. Fail to ask for the Holy Spirit (Luke 11:13)

God wants to fill us with His life, words, thoughts, power, and will. All we need to do is ask and receive of Him! The more we earnestly desire His Presence in our lives, the more our lives will be open channels for His love to flow through.

So here in Ephesians 5:18 Paul tells us that the key to living the Christian life is to *"be filled with the Spirit."* Actually, what he is saying in the original language is a little more commanding—"be *continually* filled with the Spirit." The point is: This is something we need to be doing all the time. We ought to ask Him to fill us with His Spirit, and to keep filling us every day so that our lives will be a witness of His to those around us. But how can we tell for sure that we are yielding to the Lord? How do we know that it is His life and not ours that is on display at any given time?

THREE WAYS TO TELL IF YOU ARE YIELDED

Paul identifies three ways in which we can tell whether we are truly yielded to the Holy Spirit. He says,

> Be filled with the Spirit, speaking to one another in psalms and hymns and spiritual songs, singing and making melody in your heart to the Lord, giving thanks always for all things to God the Father in the name of our Lord Jesus Christ, submitting to one another in the fear of God.
>
> —EPHESIANS 5:18–21

The three areas that he focuses on here are:

1. Our Speech

Speaking to one another in psalms and hymns and spiritual songs, singing and making melody in [our hearts] to the Lord (verse 19).

2. Our Attitude

Giving thanks always for all things to God the Father in the name of our Lord Jesus Christ (verse 20).

3. Our Relationships

Submitting to one another in the fear of God (verse 21).

Since the Holy Spirit empowers us to be witnesses for Christ, it makes sense that His influence would be evident in such practical ways. These three aspects of our daily lives (speech, attitude, and relationships) reflect what is in our hearts, and reveal whether we are yielded to the Spirit. J. Oswald Sanders wrote about this, saying,

> The real marks of the fullness of the Spirit do not consist in certain emotional states, exalted feelings, ecstatic utterances, or in signs and visions, [but] in very practical effects in life and service. These marks are readily discernible by the observer, and are not capable of counterfeit . . . nor do they merely center around and minister to the selfish enjoyment of the believer. Their sole object is to glorify Christ in the details of life and service, and to minister to the enjoyment of others. The Spirit-filled life is essentially an out-flowing life . . .[2]

1. Our Speech

What comes out of our mouths is a reflection of what is in our hearts, so a good way to tell whether we are yielded to the influence of the Holy Spirit is by our conversation. The book of Proverbs is especially full of exhortation on the proper use of the "tongue." When we are yielded to the Spirit, our speech will be graceful, melodies of praise will fill our hearts, and our words will be life-giving and edifying. Those around us will be encouraged, and their spirits will be uplifted. In contrast, when we are not yielded to the Spirit, our speech will be impetuous and characterized by careless remarks. We will tend to say whatever comes to mind, without considering the effect that our words have on others. We can all recall a time when we blurted out an off-the-cuff remark, only to moan moments later, "I can't believe I just said that!"

Lying (even stretching the truth) is another indication that we are not yielded to the Spirit. While most of us do not live a deceitful lifestyle, if we were really honest, we would have to admit that we lie a whole lot more than we would have others believe. Think about how easy it is to color the truth, just a little, in order to show ourselves in a better light—or how we tend to exaggerate a story from one telling to the next. Whenever we embellish the truth, it becomes a lie. Rationalization is yet another form of lying; we are really lying to ourselves at that point, trying to justify our behavior in order to feel better about it. But when we are under the influence of the Holy Spirit, He will prompt us to speak the truth at all times.

We can also avoid a lot of trouble by allowing the Holy Spirit to teach us the art of not speaking. Socrates once had a student apply to his school of oratory who was so talkative that he told the student, "I'm going to have to charge you double." When he asked Socrates why, he replied, "Because I've got to teach you two arts, first, how to speak and then, how not to speak." When we are under the influence of the Holy Spirit, He will guard our mouths and keep us from danger. The following story illustrates this point:

> There was a little bird that had gotten a late start on flying south for the winter and it got so cold that he froze up and fell to the ground. While he was lying there, shivering to death in a cold pasture, a cow happened by and suddenly the little bird was covered in a pile of warm manure. So he started to thaw out and as he began to warm up he started chirping. A nearby cat happened to hear the bird's song, and he set out to investigate. When he found the bird, he dug him out of the manure, and ate him up!

The moral of this story (I promise there is one) is this:

- First, not everyone who drops manure on you is your enemy! (Learn to discern between detractors and those who want the best for you.)

- Second, not everyone who digs you out of the manure is your friend! (Listening to flatterers will always lead to ruin.)

- Third (and this is the most important point), when you are in the manure, keep your mouth shut! (Foolishness is most often proven with the tongue.)

Words are powerful. We can use them either to build up and encourage or to tear down and destroy. They can comfort, or they can grieve. They can inflict pain, or they can renew hope. We bear a weighty responsibility to one another for the words that we speak. That is why Paul says that we ought to be *"speaking to one another in psalms and hymns and spiritual songs, singing and making melody in [our hearts] to the Lord"* (Ephesians 5:19).

The words that we bring forth offer insight into our hearts and prove whether we are yielded to the Holy Spirit. So, when it comes to our speech, we need to wait on the Lord to give us that perfect opportunity to say the right word at the right time. It is then that our words will be like *"apples of gold in settings of silver"* (Proverbs 25:11). When we are under the influence of the Holy Spirit, our words will have a powerful effect for good in the lives of others.

2. Our Attitude

Another sure indication of how yielded we are to the Holy Spirit is revealed by our attitudes. Just like our speech, our attitudes reflect the condition of our hearts. A right attitude is the direct result of a thankful heart. Paul says that we should be *"giving thanks always for all things"* (Ephesians 5:20). Why is thankfulness so important? When we are thankful for all things, it acknowledges that we are trusting God's plan, even when it is not clear how it is going to work out. But when we grumble and complain about our circumstances, we are not only being disobedient to the Word of God, we are also demonstrating a lack of trust and an unwillingness to yield the control of our lives fully to Him. Grumbling and complaining should have no place in the life of a believer. In fact Jude 15–16 mentions grumblers and complainers among the list of evildoers whose deeds will one day be judged and punished by God. If we are trusting God, we will be able to be thankful in all things.

In addition to grumbling and complaining, an unthankful attitude reveals itself in frustration, anger, and all sorts of ill-tempered responses to the challenges of life. We can measure the level of thankfulness in our own lives by considering the following:

- Am I quicker to blame God for my problems than I am to thank Him for His faithfulness?

- Do I lash out at those around me when things are not going my way?

- Do I come down heavy on others for their mistakes, or am I gracious and understanding when others fall short of my expectations?

- Do I ever punch the wall, slam the phone, or kick the dog when I am having a bad day?

Romans 1:21 cautions us about the impact that an unthankful attitude can have upon our lives: *"Although they knew God, they did not glorify Him as God, nor were thankful, but became futile in their thoughts, and their foolish hearts were darkened."* The end result of an unthankful attitude is futility and foolishness.

Being unthankful is profoundly shortsighted as well. One day I sat down and made a list of the five worst things that had ever happened to me. As I thought back on those difficult times, I was amazed how in every one of those instances God had turned seemingly bad situations into His blessings for my life. With God, we really can afford to be thankful in all things!

I know this is a challenge for most of us. At times we tend to jump to conclusions and judge matters too quickly. We need to be like that wise old farmer who lost his horse one day. When his friends came by to comfort him, they found that he was not upset at all. He said to them, "Say not that this is bad, for who knows, it may turn out to be a good thing."

Well, sure enough, a few days later the horse returned and brought with him a herd of wild horses. When his friends came by, this time to congratulate him, he was not celebrating at all. Instead, he said to them, "Say not that this is good, for who knows, it may turn out to be a bad thing."

Soon afterward, while his son was taming one of those wild horses, he accidentally fell and broke his leg. Once again the farmer's friends came to comfort him, and much to their surprise his attitude had not changed. He told them now, as he had told them before, "Say not that this is bad, for who knows, it may turn out to be a good thing."

As his son's leg was healing, war was declared, and all the young men were drafted into service. However, because of his broken leg, the farmer's son was not eligible to fight. Once again all the farmer's friends came by, only this time they understood, and said to him, "Say not that this is good."

This story illustrates the importance of not judging anything before its time. The events in life that seem the worst may actually turn out to be the best things that ever happen to us. So remember, "Say not that this is good, or bad," but know one thing for certain: our lives are in the hands of a loving God whose purposes and plans are always for our good. That is why thankfulness is one of the greatest expressions of trust. Those who thank the Lord, even before they see His plans unfold, will be comforted by the Presence and the promises of God. Their lives will become firmly established as they yield to the Holy Spirit, allowing Him to rule their attitudes.

Regardless of what is going on in our lives, we should never make an excuse for an unthankful or bad attitude. The only right way to handle an attitude like that is to confess it as sin and repent. If we try to justify and rationalize inappropriate behavior, it will only result in hardening our hearts even more toward the God who loves us and wants the best for us. So, what we should do instead is ask Him to forgive us and fill us with His Spirit. Truly we can, and should, give thanks to God in all things, because in doing so we will know that His power is working within us, helping us to persevere for the glory of God.

3. Our Relationships

One of the greatest proofs of whether or not we are yielded to the influence of the Holy Spirit is our relationships. Selfishness is the root of all conflict. Left unchecked, selfishness will eat away and destroy every bond of friendship we have, including our marriage.

James 3:16 says, *"Where envy and self-seeking exist, confusion and every evil thing are there."* So, when we are selfish, seeking to have our way in a situation, we are definitely not yielded to the Holy Spirit. In Ephesians 5:21, Paul draws our attention now to the fact that when we are filled with the Spirit it will affect the way we relate to each other. He says we ought to be *"submitting to one another in the fear of God."*

Whether or not we are filled with the Spirit, therefore, can easily be seen in how submitted we are to one another. That is why our relationships are a good measure of how surrendered we are to His Lordship. Just imagine what the world would be like if we were all living in submission to one another in the fear of the Lord. We would never need to be concerned about our own welfare. We would each be concerned only with fulfilling the role to which God has called us. In doing so, we would be meeting the needs of those around us, and similarly, they would be meeting our needs. That is the way God has designed His body to function. If we were all fulfilling our part, every need in the body of Christ would be met.

I believe one of the greatest examples we have in the Bible of this type of godly submission can be seen in the life of Abram. At a time when strife arose between his herdsmen and those of his nephew Lot, Abram handled the situation by giving Lot first choice over all the land. Instead of seeking after his own interests, Abram gave his nephew preference, telling him,

> Please let there be no strife between you and me. . . .
> If you take the left, then I will go to the right; or, if
> you go to the right, then I will go to the left.
>
> —GENESIS 13:8–9

Only someone who is living in the fear of the Lord could graciously submit the welfare of his or her life to another person in the way Abram does here. Remember too that Abram did not have the benefit (like we do today) of the indwelling Holy Spirit to help him. Therefore, since we do have His power within us, how submitted we are in our relationships is a good demonstration of whether we are filled with the Spirit.

Abram knew that his life was in God's hands. So when Lot chose the best portion for himself, Abram submitted to that choice because he trusted God. He did not argue with Lot. But when Lot was gone, the Lord spoke to him once again, saying:

W hat blessing and freedom we forfeit when we fail to recognize and take ownership of the promises that God has made to us in Christ.

Lift your eyes now and look from the place where you are—northward, southward, eastward, and westward; for all the land which you see I give to you and your descendants forever. And I will make your descendants as the dust of the earth; so that if a man could number the dust of the earth, then your descendants also could be numbered. Arise, walk in the land through its length and its width, for I give it to you.

—GENESIS 13:14–17

It is far better to have full possession of whatever God gives us than to grasp what we think is best for ourselves. By nature we tend to think the worst of each other. That is why we spend so much time protecting our own self-interests. So, Abram is an example to us here in that he owned only the promises of God. And in the end, he gained everything: even the portion of land that Lot had chosen was given to Abram and his descendents by the Lord. Lot lost everything in the end though, even his own family, because he allowed strife and selfishness to rule his life. What blessing and freedom we forfeit when we fail to recognize and take ownership of the promises that God has made to us in Christ.

Without a doubt, we all encounter difficult people in our lives: individuals who challenge us greatly in this area of submission. But we need to realize that even when other people bring strife and difficulty into our lives, God is worthy of our trust. We will lose only if we allow pride and selfishness to get in the way of trusting Him. Fighting for and demanding our own way will only serve to destroy any hope of bringing about peaceful resolutions to difficult situations. The more we try to win, the more embittered we will become. It is only as we willingly lay our lives aside, allowing the Holy Spirit to fill us with His love for others, that we will be able to be witnesses for Christ in all our relationships. In 1 John 3:16 we read, *"By this we know love, because He laid down His life for us. And we also ought to lay down our lives for the brethren."* It takes sacrifice to really love someone, and we cannot do that unless we are continually filled with the Spirit.

CONFIRMING EVIDENCE

> The business of living a truly Christian life is too exacting in its requirements, too lofty in its ideals, for us to engage in it alone. We need a partner . . . a partner who has adequate resources at his disposal.[3]
>
> —*J. Oswald Sanders*

It is impossible to truly live the Christian life without His help, so we need to be willing to ask for, and receive His Spirit. Indeed, confirmation of His life in us is most clearly evidenced by our speech, our attitudes, and our relationships. A Christian who is not filled with the Spirit will display very little self-control in these areas. It is only as we get serious about our desire to live lives that are truly yielded to the Lord that we will see a difference in the way we actually live. That is because only as we are filled with His Spirit do we fully realize the degree of our own self-centeredness and have the power to change.

When we are under His influence we will find the freedom, purpose, joy, and love that He intends for us. We will speak godly words, display godly attitudes, and submit lovingly to those around us. Another confirmation of His life in us is that God will pour His gifts out upon us as we yield to Him on a daily basis. The gifts of the Spirit are to be employed with love and in serving one another. The more we yield our lives to Him, the more He can use us, empower us, and give us whatever gifts we need in order to fulfill the calling He has placed on our lives.

If we were all to really live with such total abandon to the Lord, I believe that we would see revival once again in the church. We would sense His holiness and His nearness, and we would see an authentic outpouring of the gifts of the Spirit. There would be words of wisdom, words of knowledge, prophecy, tongues and their interpretation, miracles, healing, giving, leading, serving, mercy, and more—all given as He wills to those who are waiting on Him.

> Who can measure the stream of blessing that flows from the life of one who allows the Spirit of God to have His way?

It has been said that the greatness of a man's power is the measure of his surrender. Indeed, who can measure the stream of blessing that flows from the life of one who allows the Spirit of God to have His way? General William Booth (founder of the Salvation Army) was asked once, "What is the secret of your great success?" He answered:

> God has had all there was of me. There have been men with greater brains, greater opportunities than I, but from the day I had a vision of what God could do with poor old London, I made up my mind that God would have all there was of William Booth.[4]

General Booth presented his body a living sacrifice, and as a result, God was able to do a great work in him. Consider the following in your own life:

- Does God have all there is of you?
- What is the measure of your surrender?

- Do you have a vision of what He could do in your community?

- What are you doing with the opportunities that you have been given today—are you making the most of them?

Personally, I want to be sure that I am living under His influence all the time. I don't want to waste even a moment on anything else. I want the fire in my heart to burn brightly for Him every day, and I want His gracious Presence to be more of a reality in my life today than it was yesterday. I want to be sensitive to His promptings, and I want to be open and teachable. And the simplest way for me to know whether I am yielded to His Spirit or not is to examine my words, my attitudes, and my relationships.

When we stand in the Presence of the Lord one day, we will realize that the arguments we won, the bad attitudes we justified, and the times that others wronged us really never mattered. All that will matter on that day is the Lord's view of how we lived our lives. Were we submitted unto His Lordship, or did we allow the dictates of our flesh to overrule His will in our lives? Quite frankly, what He thinks should be all that matters to us today as well. If on that day, when we finally meet the Lord face to face, we want to hear Him say, *"Well done, good and faithful servant. . . . Enter into the joy of your lord"* (Matthew 25:21), then what we need to remember today is that it is the Holy Spirit who keeps us until that time.

> Now to Him who is able to keep you from stumbling, and to present you faultless before the presence of His glory with exceeding joy, to God our Savior, who alone is wise, be glory and majesty, dominion and power, both now and forever. Amen.
>
> —JUDE 24–25

Chapter Four Study Guide

THE MARK OF A YIELDED LIFE

◆ ◆ ◆

1. What is the three-part role of the Holy Spirit in a believer's life?

   a. _____

   _____

   b. _____

   _____

   c. _____

   _____

2. What do we need to do in order for Him to accomplish this?

   _____

   _____

3. In Ephesians 5:18, Paul is really illuminating the difference between the world's influence and the influence of the Holy Spirit. Make a list of any areas of your life where you think that the world's influence is greater than that of the Holy Spirit. Be specific.

   _____

   _____

4. Paul tells us in Ephesians 5:18, *"Do not be drunk with wine, in which is dissipation."* What does dissipation mean?

   _____

   _____

5. In thinking back on your answer to question four, what part of your life is being wasted (dissipated)?

_____

_____

_____

_____

_____

As you reflect on this, offer a prayer of commitment, asking the Lord to help you to begin to yield that area of your life over to the power of the Holy Spirit.

6. What three things do we need to do to in order to stay filled with the Holy Spirit? Fill in the blanks.

a. We must _____ to Him.

b. We must _____ with the Lord's changing us and making us more into His image.

c. We must _____ the things in our lives that are hindering our fellowship with the Lord.

Here is a simple way to remember these three important elements in maintaining a Spirit-controlled relationship.

Spirit:	Submit
Controlled:	Cooperate
Relationship:	Recognize

7. What four things highlighted in this chapter could hinder your fellowship with the Lord? Give a practical example of each one.

    a. _____

    _____

    b. _____

    _____

    c. _____

    _____

    d. _____

    _____

8. In Ephesians 5:18–21, Paul identifies three aspects of our daily lives that reflect whether our hearts are fully yielded. Write the key phrases from this passage that identify these three areas.

    a. _____

    _____

    b. _____

    _____

    c. _____

    _____

9. The condition of our hearts are reflected by our speech, our attitudes, and our relationships. Under each category below, write what new insight or understanding you now have from the discussion in this chapter regarding this statement. Now make it personal. What area in particular do you want God to change in you in each category? Be specific.

Your Speech:

_____

_____

_____

Your Attitudes:

_____

_____

_____

Your Relationships:

_____

_____

_____

As you close this study in prayer, ask the Lord to help you yield your life to the Holy Spirit more fully so that the fire in your heart would burn more brightly for Him.

Years ago, at a conference, I heard a speaker declare that the greatest capacity of man was his ability to contain God. He was preaching on 2 Corinthians 4:7, where Paul says, "We have this treasure in earthen vessels," and was describing the glory of our bodies being the temple of the Holy Spirit. He made a very inspiring, powerful presentation and I was stirred and moved that my body should be the temple of the Holy Spirit.

But as you read on in Scriptures, you discover that the greatest capacity of man is not being a vessel that can contain God; rather, it's being a vessel through which God can be poured out to the world around us. That's the real glory!

The ultimate work of the Spirit is not merely to transform and change and empower us that we might be blessed. His ultimate work is empowering us to serve, to become effective in bringing Jesus Christ to others. God's Spirit wants to use you and me to bring the love of God to others. He wants His Spirit to flow like a torrent of living water out of our lives and into the lives of those who have yet to quench their thirst at the fountain of God.[1]

—*Chuck Smith*

TORRENTS OF LIVING WATER

In this chapter, we are going to be examining the Spirit-filled life from yet another viewpoint: the extraordinary way in which God uses a yielded life as a channel of His blessings. As we have already seen, life in the Spirit is:

- A life of choice: *Being filled with the Spirit necessitates our making a deliberate choice to yield to His influence.*

- A life of purpose: *As we are yielded to His Spirit, He empowers us to live according to His purposes.*

In addition, we will see that the Spirit-filled life is:

- A life of blessing: *He not only fills our lives, but overflows them, making our lives outlets of His blessings to those around us.*

One of the most beautiful emblems in the Bible, depicting this life-giving ministry of the Holy Spirit in the lives of God's people, is water. Water is an essential element of life. Thirst is one of the two most powerful human drives we have; our need for water is second only to our need for oxygen. We could not survive very long without either.

Today, because of its availability, most of us take water pretty much for granted, but that was not the case at the time the Scriptures were written. Primarily, the ancient biblical writers lived in desert regions where water was scarce, and drought was a constant threat to their existence. They depended continually on the Lord to provide the rains they needed. He was their source of water; He was their Source of Life. That is why water is such a magnificent picture of the life-sustaining ministry of the Holy Spirit and the relationship that God desires for us to have with Him each day. His Presence sustains our spiritual lives in much the same way water sustains our physical ones.

We see this theme reflected throughout the pages of Scripture. King David wrote in Psalm 42:1, *"As the deer pants for the water brooks, so pants my soul for You, O God. My soul thirsts for God, for the living God."* And the prophet Isaiah also wrote much about this aspect of our relationship with the Lord. In Isaiah 58:11 he said:

> The LORD will guide you continually, and satisfy your soul in drought, and strengthen your bones; you shall be like a watered garden, and like a spring of water, whose waters do not fail.

This passage in Isaiah is one of the Scriptures that God gave my wife Karen and me when we were praying about moving from California to New Jersey to begin a Bible study. It was a big step for us, but one for which God had given us a great desire. People told us that the East Coast was the "graveyard of churches," and that spiritually it was a dry, desert land. We had so many reasons not to leave the fruitful ministry we were a part of in California, but we also had this great promise from the Lord: He would go with us, guiding, strengthening, and satisfying our souls with waters that would not fail. How could we not step out in faith, believing that God had a work for us to do? So, fortified by the Word of God, we left our fellowship, friends, and family behind. And just as He promised, the Lord established a new work on the East Coast. We certainly learned that there is no desert that the Spirit of the Lord cannot turn into a fruitful abode.

LIFE-GIVING WATER

In John 7:37–38 Jesus promises that *"rivers of living water"* will flow from the hearts of all who are thirsty and come to Him. The Greek word *potamos*, which is translated "rivers" in this passage, actually means "torrents" or "floods"; it is an abundance of flowing water. This is not a gentle, tranquil, meandering brook that Jesus is talking about, but a swift and powerful river overflowing its banks. So, out of the heart (or innermost being) of all who come to Jesus will gush forth a mighty, rushing river of life-giving sustenance, filling their lives and spilling over onto the lives of others as well.

> If we believe in Jesus, it is not what we gain but what He pours through us that really counts. God's purpose is not simply to make us beautiful, plump grapes, but to make us grapes so that He may squeeze the sweetness out of us. Our spiritual life cannot be measured by success as the world measures it, but only by what God pours through us—and we cannot measure that at all.[2]
>
> —*Oswald Chambers*

As we walk in the Spirit, the Lord is interested not only in blessing us, but in using our lives as a means by which He can bless others as well.

Unfortunately though, some of us would rather be ponds than rivers. We love to accumulate all of God's blessings for our lives, but we are reluctant to let Him use our lives as channels of blessing to others. Standing water tends to become stagnant over time, however, and eventually everything in it will die. On the other hand, a flowing river is a fresh, life-sustaining environment and everything in it will thrive.

How would you describe your Christian life today? Would you say it is a fresh, life-sustaining environment, or a stagnant pond? Are there "torrents" of living water overflowing your life, or are you in a dry, desert place? If Jesus says that He can make our lives like rivers of living water, then why are so many of us still thirsty?

One undeniable cause for spiritual dryness is anxiety. Most days we have things "wired"; our lives are under control and we are not outwardly anxious about anything. But when we lie down, we find no rest as all the issues of life flood through our minds. Our souls grow restless and anxious—thirsting for God and the peace, rest, and purpose that only He can impart.

Another cause for spiritual dryness is guilt. Guilt is a weight on the soul, a burden felt continually, deep within our hearts. Guilt's only purpose is to lead us to the Lord—it cannot be quieted without a touch from Him. As with anxiety, sometimes guilt can overwhelm our souls.

God created us to be satisfied and complete only in Him.

Whatever causes us to become spiritually dry (anxiety, guilt, or any number of other issues), only God can truly quench our thirsty souls. That is the reason why, despite the many successes we have in life, we will always experience a void (a thirst within our souls) that cannot be satisfied apart from an abiding relationship with the living God. That is why Jesus invited all who are thirsty to come and drink from Him.

> When Jesus said, "If any man thirst," He was refer-ring to that deep universal thirst of man's spirit for God. It is interesting to me that some psychology textbooks identify frustration as one of the root causes of neurotic behavior. They declare that a per-son's problem often begins with frustration, that feeling that you have not attained what life is all about, that there must be more to life than what you have experienced—but what is it and how do I attain it? It is reaching out for something I am not sure of, and not finding what I am hoping for. What is frus-tration but thirst, spiritual thirst, that deep thirst in man's spirit for God?[3]
>
> —*Chuck Smith*

God created us to be satisfied and complete only in Him. The things of this world cannot meet the need we have within for a relationship with our Creator. Though we may be entertained and kept busy for a little while, eventually these things will only leave us thirsting for more. What we learn from these times of spiritual dryness is simply that we have been drinking at the wrong fountain. In His mercy, God allows dryness in our lives just so we will realize that nothing in this world (whether relationships, possessions, position, or ministry) can take His place.

We can easily err in thinking that our lives consist solely of the body (physical) and the soul (emotional). We can spend all our time seeking ways to satisfy the passions and desires that we have in these areas. However, while love, security, acceptance, food, water, and clothing are all necessary to life, even when these needs are being adequately met, something is still missing. What we fail to recognize is that essentially we are spiritual beings and none of these things can quench a spiritual thirst.

That is why Jesus invites those who are thirsty to come to Him; we each have a deep spiritual need that is satisfied only in an abiding relationship with the Lord. As we come to Jesus and yield our lives to His control, we experience the Holy Spirit as *"rivers of living water,"* refreshing not only our own thirsty souls, but overflowing into the lives of those around us.

As we come to Jesus and yield our lives to His control, we experience the Holy Spirit as "rivers of living water."

THE FEAST OF TABERNACLES

> On the last day, that great day of the feast, Jesus stood and cried out, saying, "If anyone thirsts, let him come to Me and drink. He who believes in Me, as the Scripture has said, out of his heart will flow rivers of living water." But this He spoke concerning the Spirit, whom those believing in Him would

receive; for the Holy Spirit was not yet given, because Jesus was not yet glorified.

—JOHN 7:37–39

This passage in John 7 is interesting for two reasons:

1. Because of the day Jesus chose to make this statement. The apostle John says that it was on the last and greatest day of the feast.

2. Because it is the first time Jesus ever spoke about the new relationship that His followers would have with the Holy Spirit.

So, on this very significant day Jesus is teaching them a powerful lesson about the ministry of the Holy Spirit.

Jesus spoke to the whole nation of Israel which was gathered together in Jerusalem celebrating the Feast of Tabernacles. This was a time of great national rejoicing. The Feast of Tabernacles was the last of the seven annual feasts that were established by God (Leviticus 23), and one of the three times each year that all the men of Israel were required to journey to Jerusalem (Deuteronomy 16:16). This was a day when all of God's people were represented before Him in the temple.

This feast was celebrated at the end of the fall harvest season, but it was not just a time of thanksgiving for God's people; it was also a time of remembrance. The people commemorated how God had preserved the nation for forty years in the wilderness. It was also a time for them to look forward to the final harvest, when all the nations will be gathered unto the Lord (Zechariah 14:16–19).

This feast (like all Jewish feast days) is also ripe with tradition and religious emblems symbolizing the power and Presence of God. Immediately prior to the feast days, the men of Israel would build temporary shelters for their families out of palm branches, replicating the dwellings the people would have lived in during their years of exile in the desert. They would then move out of their comfortable homes and live in these camp-style settings during the eight days of the feast, which was known in the Hebrew as *Succoth*. Chuck Smith shares some insight on this tradition in his book *Charisma vs. Charismania:*

> As tradition developed, they were to leave enough space in the roof thatches so that they could see the stars at night, to remind them that their forefathers had slept under the stars for 40 years. Also, enough space was to be left in the walls so that the wind could blow through, so they would remember that even though their fathers were exposed to the elements for 40 years, God miraculously preserved them.[4]

So these shelters, referred to as either booths or tabernacles in the Bible, served to remind God's people of some very important spiritual truths:

- The faithfulness of God in preserving His people for forty years in the desert wilderness, and their continued need for dependence on Him each day.

- The temporal nature of their lives. Even though they were living in permanent shelters in the Promised Land, their lives were just as transitory as their ancestors who lived as *"strangers and pilgrims on the earth"* (Hebrews 11:13).

These are still important lessons for God's people today. How easy it is to lose sight of God when life becomes a little bit more settled. And, how important it is for us to pause and remember His power, majesty, and faithfulness each day.

The feast days also provided an opportunity for the stories of old to be retold and handed down to the next generation. I can only imagine all the questions the children must have asked their parents during those long nights as they slept under the stars. How their vision of the Almighty must have grown as they listened to the stories of God's miraculous preservation of the nation of Israel—food from the heavens, clothing that never wore out, and the most precious of all commodities in the desert, water from a rock!

Those were thrilling days, indeed—days when the whole nation paused from the busyness of life to:

- Honor God for His past provision.

- Remember Him for His present faithfulness.

- Trust in Him for His future promises.

And on this *particular* day in the history of the nation, it was also a time of visitation and revelation, as the very Messiah that they awaited was standing in their midst.

Every day during the feast there were elaborate services performed in the temple. The ceremonial carrying of the water took place each morning. The priest, whose duty it was to fill a golden pitcher with the pristine water from the pool of Siloam, would enter the temple through the "Water Gate" amidst a joyful procession, with trumpets blasting and people chanting praises to their God. Included among those praises would have been the words of Isaiah 12:3, *"With joy you will draw water from the wells of salvation."* The most dramatic moment came as the priest poured the contents of the pitcher into the basin next to the altar, symbolizing the life-giving water that God miraculously provided for His people from a rock in the wilderness (Exodus 17:6).

> W ith joy you will draw water from the wells of salvation.

On the last day of the feast, the greatest day of all, Jesus, who Paul tells us in 1 Corinthians 10:4, is the "spiritual" Rock who provided water in the wilderness, stood, declaring these incredible words in John 7:37–38:

> "If anyone thirsts, let him come to Me and drink . . . out of his heart will flow rivers of living water."

- What incredible timing: *"On the last day, that great day."*

- What an amazing invitation: *"If anyone thirsts, let him come to Me and drink."*

- What an awesome promise: *"Rivers of living water,"* as opposed to mere pitchers that run dry.

Undoubtedly, Jesus would have had everyone's attention.

IF ANY MAN THIRSTS

Jesus' invitation is open to all who will come—it is neither an exclusive offer nor is it given as a reward for anything anyone can do. He simply says that *all* who believe may come to Him and receive of Him. Just like in the wilderness when God supplied water from a "Rock," the thirsty will continually be refreshed by an endless supply from the Lord.

Of course, He is not speaking about the same kind of physical thirst that those in the desert would have known. Water was their most pressing need—they would have quickly died without it. So God provided it for them in a miraculous way, and by doing so He also gave them a beautiful foreshadowing of the ministry of the Holy Spirit. It was a *"shadow of things to come . . . the substance [of which] is of Christ"* (Colossians 2:17). And now Jesus (the "Rock" in the wilderness) stood among them and invited them all to come and drink.

It is interesting to note that what He is saying in the original language is, *"If anyone is STILL thirsty, come to Me"* (emphasis added). I have to wonder why they would have still been thirsty. After all, they had just observed a full week of religious instruction, feasting, and fellowship. So why was Jesus saying this to them? Could it be that even this special feast, with all its religious observances, was not enough to satisfy the thirst within their hearts for God?

Religious activity cannot quench spiritual thirst because religion is man's attempt to reach God through ceremonies, rituals, and works. All the pomp and circumstance in the world, however, cannot change the truth that in ourselves we have nothing to offer God. As spiritual beings, we were made to have fellowship with our Creator. The absence of that relationship is the source of spiritual thirst. Since that is where it comes from, we cannot possibly satisfy it with anything other than His Presence. How empty their eight days of religious feasting must have seemed to Jesus; how much He must have wanted them to come and be satisfied in Him alone. That is what He wants for our life as well: that we would satisfy ourselves in His Presence alone.

Jesus is God's answer to our greatest need. At the cross He reached down and took care of the sin that separated us from Him so that we could have fellowship with Him once again. He bridged the gap for us; all we need to do is receive the grace that He so freely offers. Religion, apart from relationship, is very much like the priest's pitcher—it keeps running dry. But when we are filled with the Spirit, our lives are like flowing rivers. That is why even serving the Lord will leave us dry if we are depending on our own resources to energize our activities instead of allowing the Holy Spirit to work through us. A pastor once wrote the following thoughts to me:

In every church, during any given service there is . . .

- A single mother who feels as though she is being crushed under the weight of all her responsibilities.

- An elderly man who is frustrated and angry because of his failing health.

- A young man who is tempted by sexual sin and tormented with guilt.

- A teenager who is listening with that MTV attention span.

- A businessman who is caught in the depths of depression.

- A Sunday school teacher who is clinging to faith by a fingernail.

- A married couple who are hardly speaking at home.

- A frustrated parent looking for confidence.

- A widow whose eyes still fill with tears as her hand touches the empty seat beside her.

- A cancer patient who needs a reason to go on.
- A nurse who is exhausted from twelve-hour shifts.
- A lonely soul who is looking for companionship.
- A new Christian who wants to build his faith.
- A tired ministry leader who is longing for a boost.
- An elder in need of power.

And they all look expectantly to the man who stands up to preach.

Who dares to rise and preach in the face of such need? Who can meet such a multiplicity of expectations? Only God can, through the Person of the Holy Spirit. The power in preaching is not in the man himself or the preaching—it is the Spirit of God speaking through the preacher's faltering words, stiff outlines, and overused illustrations. God uses unworthy vessels in order to anoint hearts, persuade minds, lift spirits, comfort pain, and enlighten understanding.

As a pastor, I know that I cannot even think about ministering to God's people without the empowerment of the Holy Spirit. I need to be filled to overflowing with His life in order to live up to His call. And so do you! As Christians, you and I need His continual living water flowing through our lives.

G od has determined to use us to carry forth His life into the world.

The pool of Siloam was the water garden from which the priests drew water for the pitcher used in the temple services. This pitcher is a beautiful illustration of the yielded Christian life. Just as it was set aside to be filled with the water that was to be carried into the congregation, so our lives are the vessels that have been set aside by God to be filled with His "living water." God has determined to use us to carry forth His life into the world. Our lives and ministries, therefore, become poured-out offerings, empowered and directed by the hand of God, and used solely for His purposes and only for His glory.

Jesus' words that day held so much promise—more than all the days of religious feasting ever could. He made an offer that only He had the authority and the power to make. I could never tell you that if you came to me, I would cause rivers of life to flow from your heart. But Jesus can. He spoke like no other man, because Jesus is God. He came for that very moment. He stood and spoke to His people not to interrupt the proceedings, but to interpret them—to show them what their lives could become. Imagine not just a ceremonial pitcher of water, but an endless supply of life-giving sustenance gushing forth from their very own hearts!

What the Lord offered to them on that day two thousand years ago is the same thing that He offers to us today—all who come to Him will experience His abundant life freely flowing from their hearts. The apostle John provides the commentary for us, right in this passage, by telling us that the flowing water symbolizes the life-giving effect of the Holy Spirit in the lives of all who come to Him and drink. Jesus wanted the people to come to the true Rock. He wanted them to fix their eyes on their Source of Life.

COME TO JESUS AND DRINK

Jesus says, *"If anyone thirsts, let him come to Me and drink"* (John 7:37). This offer is for everyone who will come to Him. But what does it really mean to come to Jesus?

Coming to Jesus is, first of all, believing in what the Scriptures teach us about who He is. He says, *"He who believes in Me, as the Scripture has said"* (verse 38, emphasis added).

We come to Jesus by trusting and putting our full faith in who He is and what He has done. When we come to Him, we lean upon Him and cast the care of our souls to Him alone. We embrace Him as our personal Lord and Savior because we realize that there is nothing in us that can meet the need that He has already met in our lives. By the sacrifice of His life He has paid our sin debt in full, and reconciled us, once and for all, to God. We can have an abiding relationship with our Creator when we come to Jesus *"as the Scripture has said."*

Coming to Him, therefore, does not mean that we add Him to all the other beliefs and ideas that we hold. We cannot just put Jesus on the dashboard of our car, along with our religious medals, our Buddha, our crystals, and all our other lucky charms. Coming to Jesus means counting the cost and making a clear decision. We are choosing Him above all gods because there is no other God. Jesus is the only One who has ever overcome death. The invitation He extends is for us to join Him and to partake of His divine nature. Faith in Jesus Christ alone is what saves our souls from eternal destruction.

That is what it means to come to Jesus. Even Christians who are saved and walking with the Lord can forget the simplicity of the gospel message. We can get caught up in religion once again. Jesus is saying to us, *"Keep coming to Me and I will keep refreshing you."*

Jesus is not offering us another religious system. He is offering us eternal life—His own life! Coming to Jesus is about abandoning all else and choosing Him. It is about realizing that nothing in this world can take His place.

> We cannot just put Jesus on the dashboard of our car, along with our religious medals, our Buddha, our crystals, and all our other lucky charms.

- Are you weary and feeling somewhat crushed under the load of all your responsibilities?—*Come to Jesus!*

- Are you frustrated and angry over diminishing strength and energy due to failing health?—*Come to Jesus!*

- Are you a tired servant, an exhausted church worker, or an elder in need of power to persevere?—*Come to Jesus!*

- Are you defeated by sin, swallowed up with guilt, or in need of personal revival?—*Come to Jesus!*

Whether from confusion, depression, discouragement, frustration, loneliness, fear, or doubt—whatever it is that has dried out your soul—come to Jesus. Put everything else aside, and drink deeply of the resource He provides. Let Him satisfy you and you will experience His abundant life flowing from the depths of your heart—He *will* change your life.

EXPERIENCING RIVERS OF LIVING WATER

Jesus said that out of the heart of all who believe in Him would *"flow rivers of living water."* A river derives its power from its source. The force of that power is what overcomes obstacles that hinder or impede the river's flow. Like a river, the power we need to live the Christian life flows from a Source as well. The Holy Spirit is the Source of power in our lives. We need to dive in and be willing to "flow" with God, keeping our focus on the Source of our power and not the obstacles along the way. The question is: Have you waded fully into that river of life?

Ezekiel chapter 47 offers a vivid picture of the total abandonment to the moving of the Spirit that God desires. In it we read how the water flowing from the temple of the Lord is being measured in various places. The first time it is measured Ezekiel says, *"The water came up to my ankles"* (verse 3). Ankle-deep water has very little impact on a person. Even if it were a mighty rushing current, he would still be able to resist its influence completely and maintain his own course. How like many Christians today who are happy to be saved by grace, but still desire to satisfy themselves in the world. They are only ankle deep.

Next Ezekiel walks out a little deeper where he says, *"The water came up to my knees"* (verse 4). In knee-deep water you will experience more of the water's powerful force and your walk will become a little more cautious. When you are knee-deep, there is a little less of self showing through, but you can still resist and go your own way pretty easily.

The third time, he ventures out deeper still, where he says, *"The water came up to my waist"* (verse 4). It would be a little bit more difficult to resist the influence of the river at this point, but it would still not necessarily overpower us. However, waist-deep water is a direct challenge to our strength. The deeper we go, the more obvious our own limitations become.

Finally he says, *"I could not cross; for the water was too deep"* (verse 5). This time the river was over his head and he was submerged in it. In a river that is deep and powerful, a person has no choice but to be carried along irresistibly in its mighty current.

Understand this: the Holy Spirit in your life is just like a mighty rushing river. So let me ask you: Where are you in that river? Are you merely dipping your toes into the water, sensing His Presence, but not allowing Him to move your life very much? Or, perhaps you have ventured out and are experiencing more of His power, but a lot of self is still showing—you are not fully yielded, but still ruling your own life. Let me exhort you strongly at this point that unless you are content with nothing less than total submersion into that river, you will never really experience the fullness of life that God wants to give you.

> And it shall be that every living thing that moves, wherever the rivers go, will live.
>
> —EZEKIEL 47:9

I know that I do not want to be a Christian who is just getting my feet wet; I do not want to be a Christian who is depending on my own resources. I want to be a Christian whose life is fully immersed in His. I want to be a Christian who is yielded completely to the influence of the Holy Spirit and experiencing the abundant life that I have been promised in Christ! The true Christian experience is one in which self is progressively giving way to the Spirit of God working within.

> *Oh, the bitter shame and sorrow,*
> *That a time could ever be,*

When I let the Savior's pity
    Plead in vain, and proudly answered—
"All of self, and none of Thee."

Yet He found me; I beheld Him
    Bleeding on the cursed tree;
Heard Him pray, "Forgive them, Father,"
    And my wistful heart said faintly—
"Some of self, and some of Thee."

Day by day His tender mercy
    Healing, helping, full and free
Sweet and strong, and ah! so patient,
    Brought me lower, while I whispered,
"Less of self, and more of Thee."

Higher than the highest heavens
    Deeper than the deepest sea,
Lord, Thy love at last hath conquered,
    Grant me now my soul's petition,
"None of self, and all of Thee."[5]

—Theodore Monod

Chapter Five Study Guide

TORRENTS OF LIVING WATER

◆ ◆ ◆

1. According to the quote by Chuck Smith in the opening portion of this chapter, what is the ultimate work of the Holy Spirit in our lives?

_____

_____

2. Why is water such a magnificent picture of the life-sustaining relationship that God desires for us to have with Him each day?

_____

_____

3. In John 7:38, Jesus promised that *"rivers of living water"* would flow from the hearts of all those who would come to Him and drink. What does the Greek word *potamos*, which is translated as "rivers" in the New King James Version, literally mean?

_____

_____

4. Does this surprise you? Why or why not?

_____

_____

5. In this chapter, Oswald Chambers is quoted as saying, "Our spiritual life cannot be measured by success as the world measures it, but only by what God pours through us—and we cannot

measure that at all." Give a practical example of what this "pouring through us" looks like.

_____

_____

6. What are some of the causes of spiritual thirst?

_____

_____

7. What are you doing to satisfy your thirst? Are you seeking to satisfy it in any way other than through an abiding relationship with the Lord?

_____

_____

8. What was the significance of Jesus' statement in John 7:37–38, *"If anyone thirsts, let him come to Me and drink. . . . out of his heart will flow rivers of living water"* on the last day of the Feast of Tabernacles?

_____

_____

9. Where does spiritual dryness come from and how do we fill it?

_____

_____

10. What does coming to Jesus really mean?

_____

_____

11. Review the passage in Ezekiel 47 that portrays a vivid picture of total abandonment to the moving of the Spirit in our lives. The Holy Spirit in your life is like this mighty rushing river. Where are you in relation to that river? Are you the one dipping your toes in or have you maybe gone a little further? Explain.

_____

_____

12. Where would you place yourself today on the graph below?

Ankle Deep	Knee Deep	Waist Deep	Over Your Head Carried Away

As you close this study in prayer, ask the Lord to fill you to overflowing until you are carried away in Him.

In many cases, misconceptions concerning the Spirit and ignorance of His work are responsible for weakness and ineffectiveness in Christian life and labor. If only the Spirit could come into His own, lives would be rich in fruitfulness and fragrant with the perfume of Christ. By realizing all that the third person of the Trinity has for us, facts of promise could become factors of power.[1]

—*Herbert Lockyer*

CHAPTER 6

TEST ALL THINGS

We have already looked at who the Holy Spirit is, why He is an important part of our Christian lives, and how we can tell whether or not we are under His influence. From the pages of Scripture, we have seen some of the promises, benefits, and examples of being filled with and empowered by the Holy Spirit. Why then is the Person and ministry of the Holy Spirit one of the most controversial subjects in the church today? Why does so much misunderstanding abound regarding His rightful place?

In his book, *Living Water*, Chuck Smith writes, *"I am convinced that the greatest need in the church today is a renewal of the teaching on the subject of the Holy Spirit."*[2] If we desire to live a Spirit-filled life, then we need to become familiar with what the Bible teaches about the Holy Spirit. The only way to insure against the danger of deception is by searching the Scriptures ourselves. Believers can know if something is a legitimate work of the Spirit by simply testing it against the Word of God. The confusion that exists today within the body of Christ is proof that Satan's strategy to prevent Christians from understanding what the Bible says about the Holy Spirit's rightful place in their lives has been a huge success.

> Satan has two methods of procedure in dealing with truth. First, he seeks to hide the vision. . . . Then Satan's method is that of patronage and falsification. He endeavors to take it out of its true proportion and turn it into deadly error.[3]
>
> —*Herbert Lockyer*

What better way to prevent the furtherance of the gospel than to cause confusion and division regarding the Holy Spirit's role in the life of the church?

TWO DIFFERING VIEWPOINTS

This confusion is evident by the wide variety of opinions prevailing in Christian circles today regarding how the Holy Spirit operates. Simply stated, on the one hand we have those who emphasize their own "experience" as being the measure of whether something is a real move of the Spirit, while others feel just as strongly that the Holy Spirit no longer manifests Himself today in the same ways that He did when the church was being established. However, both of these extremes fall short because they are not founded on the clear teaching of Scripture.

We make a big mistake by assuming that just because we have an emotional experience (where we feel "moved" by something), it was the Holy Spirit who moved us.

DISCERNING THE SPIRITS

Those who go overboard, emphasizing experiences, are in danger of being deceived by their own emotions and feelings. This is not to say that we will never sense the Holy Spirit's Presence moving in very personal and profound ways. We definitely will. But if our experiences become the foundation of our relationship with the Lord—to the point they actually supercede the authority of Scripture—that is a huge problem. Without a scriptural basis, experiences, no matter how real, cannot and should not be trusted.

Yet many Christians are deceived because they do not test their experiences against the Word of God. That is why we need to be grounded in His Word so that we can know if what we are experiencing is valid. We make a big mistake by assuming that just because we have an emotional experience (where we feel "moved" by something), it was the Holy Spirit who moved us. Cults are full of those who have experienced real things, but none of them are from God.

How often I have heard Christians say that the "Spirit" moved them to take a certain course of action—even though it violated a clear teaching of Scripture. If something is not biblical, then we are not being led of the Spirit of God to do it, no matter how strongly we may feel. It is really that simple. He will never move us to act outside of what has been clearly revealed in His Word. Christians go wrong when they rely on their feelings and experiences without testing them against the Word of God. The Bible exhorts us in this, saying:

> Do not believe every spirit, but test the spirits, whether they are of God; because many false prophets have gone out into the world.
>
> —1 JOHN 4:1

Another way to test whether an experience is a legitimate work of the Holy Spirit is to simply ask yourself this question: Where does it draw my attention? Unfortunately, much of what we see publicly demonstrated and attributed to the work of the Holy Spirit today is really nothing more than hype and sensationalism—calling attention to man rather than to God. When the Holy Spirit moves among His people, the purpose is always to draw attention to *Jesus*. Jesus told His disciples that when the Holy Spirit came, He would:

- *"Teach you all things, and bring to your remembrance all things that I said to you."* (John 14:26)

- *"Testify of Me."* (John 15:26)

- *"Convict the world of sin, and of righteousness, and of judgment."* (John 16:8)

- *"Guide you into all truth."* (John 16:13)

- *"Glorify Me."* (John 16:14)

Therefore, anything that draws attention to an individual, or to a particular sign or wonder that has occurred, and not to Jesus, is not a real move of the Spirit at all. It is just a work of the flesh. When we are truly in His Presence, we are not focusing on ourselves or our experiences. Instead, our unworthiness in light of His holiness is what is brought into full view, producing in us a deep sense of humility.

Indeed, one of the marks of a real encounter with the Spirit of God is that it produces humility in our lives, which is the opposite of so much of what we see done in His name today. Andrew Murray wrote, *"Humility is the bloom and beauty of holiness. The chief mark of counterfeit holiness is the lack of humility."*[4] The pages of Scripture are marked by this kind of genuine humility in the Presence of God:

- The prophet Isaiah was one of the most eloquent speakers of all time, yet when He was in the Presence of the Lord, he proclaimed himself to be *"a man of unclean lips"* (Isaiah 6:5).

- Jesus, in Matthew 11:11, said that of all those born of women there was none *"greater than John the Baptist,"* yet John told others that he was unworthy even to carry Jesus' sandals (Matthew 3:11).

- The apostle Peter was a skilled fisherman, yet when he witnessed the incredible catch of fish that was netted at the Lord's command, he fell down before Him, saying, *"Depart from me, for I am a sinful man, O Lord!"* (Luke 5:8).

We also see this mark of genuine humility demonstrated throughout the history of the church, proving that a real manifestation of the Spirit is accompanied by great humility. One such demonstration occurred during the great Welsh revival in 1904. Rees Howell (a man God used greatly during that time) recorded what happened one night when the Holy Spirit moved during a prayer meeting. He writes:

> An awesome sense of God's nearness began to steal over the whole college. There was a solemn expectancy . . . we only wanted to spend our time in prayer and supplication—conscious that God's hand was upon us—conscious that He was about to do something. God was there—yet we felt we were still waiting for Him to come. And in the days that followed, He came. He did not come like a mighty rushing wind. But gradually the person of the Holy Ghost filled all our thoughts, His presence filled all the place and His light seemed to penetrate all hidden recesses of our hearts. . . . It was a "face to face" experience. And when we saw Him we knew we had never really seen Him before. We said like Job, "I have heard of thee by the hearing of my ear: but now my eye sees thee" and like him we cried, "wherefore I abhor myself and repent in dust and ashes."
>
> In light of His purity, it was not so much sin we saw as self. We saw pride and self motives underlying everything we had ever done. Lust and self-pity were discovered in places where we had never suspected them. The Spirit impressed on us, "Who is in control of your life, Me or you?"[5]

We saw pride and self motives underlying everything we had ever done.

Genuine humility makes way for both the power and glory of God to be manifested in, and known through, our lives. Christ's life is the greatest demonstration of glory, humility, and power that this world will ever see. He was:

- Conceived by the power of the Holy Spirit: *"The Holy Spirit will come upon you, and the power of the Highest will overshadow you"* (Luke 1:35).

- Baptized by the power of the Holy Spirit: *"The Holy Spirit descended in bodily form like a dove upon Him"* (Luke 3:22).

- Filled and led by the power of the Holy Spirit: *"Jesus, being filled with the Holy Spirit . . . was led by the Spirit into the wilderness"* (Luke 4:1).

- Empowered for ministry by the Holy Spirit: *"Jesus returned in the power of the Spirit. . . . And He taught in their synagogues, being glorified by all"* (Luke 4:14–15).

- Resurrected from the dead by the power of the Holy Spirit: *"The Spirit of Him who raised Jesus from the dead"* (Romans 8:11).

The power of the Holy Spirit is truly amazing! Scripture, the annals of church history, and the reality of Christ's life all testify of His power. The apostle Paul tells us that our lives can be testimonies of His as well, *"He who raised Christ from the dead will also give life to your mortal bodies through His Spirit who dwells in you"* (Romans 8:11).

The question we need to ask ourselves is: Why would God desire for us to have this power in our daily lives? What purpose does it serve? One pastor shared this comment regarding the purpose of the Holy Spirit's power:

> When you have steam in a steam engine its purpose is to drive the engine—to move it somewhere. But, all some people want to do is to use the steam to make the whistle blow. They are making a lot of noise, but they are not going anywhere. They are just drawing attention to themselves.

Some people just want to sound the whistle! They want the emotions, the feelings, and the Holy Spirit "goose bumps." The experience becomes the goal and that is dangerous. Because what is attributed to a move of the Spirit is oftentimes nothing more than just a cloak for the flesh: a superficial layer of spirituality, but it is going nowhere. If our Christianity is based on our experiences, and not on Jesus, then it has nothing to do with the power of the Holy Spirit.

God does not give us power for our amusement. It is not so we can sit in our churches and feel good about ourselves. God wants to empower our lives, making them a testimony to the lost world around us—a testimony of who Jesus is and what He can do. God gives us power so that we can fulfill the plans that He has for us, overcome sin in our lives, and behave wisely in every situation. God's power in our lives is not meant for our own experience; it is meant to bring Him glory.

> **If our Christianity is based on our experiences, and not on Jesus, then it has nothing to do with the power of the Holy Spirit.**

> We want to get possession of the power and use it; God wants the power to get possession of us and use us.[6]
>
> —*Andrew Murray*

God has a specific purpose for each of our lives and wants to move us in that direction. He wants us to let go of our own emotional desires and earthly pursuits and set our minds on higher things. He wants to use us to further His kingdom, not just sound the whistle. He wants the world to see Jesus.

A FORM OF GODLINESS

In contrast to those who go overboard with the emphasis on "experience," others hold to the opposite extreme. They feel that the signs and wonders that defined the early church in the book of Acts are no longer necessary today, and that the more "spectacular" (or obvious) gifts of the Spirit, such as prophecy, tongues, interpretation of tongues, miracles, and healings are no longer active in the body of Christ. In their opinion, those things were only needed in order to authenticate the claims of Christ as the Messiah and to establish unity among the first believers. They reason that since this work has been accomplished and we now have a thriving Christian church, those kinds of manifestations and outpourings of the Spirit are just not needed anymore.

It is important to acknowledge the fact that many fine Christians hold this doctrinal viewpoint. Even though they would not deny their need for dependence upon the supernatural empowerment of the Holy Spirit altogether, they do limit Him by believing that not every gift is operational today. All the gifts of the Spirit are supernatural, but the spectacular, they believe, have ceased.

The debate over whether certain gifts of the Spirit are still in existence today is really a topic for another discussion. I assure you, many large volumes have already been written on the subject. But for the sake of our purpose (yielding to His influence), I want to state three simple reasons that I believe prove all the gifts of the Spirit are still in operation today:

1. There is no scriptural basis for believing that these gifts are no longer valid.

2. Church history confirms that these gifts continue to be in operation.

3. Jesus' warning (Matthew 24:24) about *false* signs and wonders was completely unnecessary if *all* signs and wonders were going to cease.

When we can reason away God's gifts, we can easily deny that His power is at work in our world today. This impression is the real danger of this viewpoint because it fosters a greater dependency on our own strengths and abilities, while creating a lack of dependency upon the Holy Spirit.

In 2 Timothy 3:5, Paul warned young Timothy about those who would come in among the believers and try to deceive them. He said Timothy would recognize them because they would have a *"form of godliness but [would deny] its power."* In other words, they would look and sound really spiritual, but their empty religious emblems and rituals would reveal to all who truly know the Lord that their lives were void of a living relationship with Jesus Christ. Charles Spurgeon wrote about this in *Lectures to My Students:*

> People go to their place of worship and sit down comfortably, and think they must be Christians. . . . Thousands are congratulating themselves, and even blessing God that they are devout worshippers, when at the same time they are living in an unregenerate Christless state, having the form of godliness, but denying the power thereof.[7]

Having a form of godliness is sometimes even more dangerous than not having any knowledge of God at all. In I Samuel 4 the Lord allowed His people to lose a battle with the godless Philistines in order to teach them this same lesson. The people had strayed from their relationship with God. Instead of walking obediently in His Presence, they were putting their trust in empty religious rituals and symbols. They looked godly on the outside, but they were devoid of His power. When they found themselves facing the Philistine army—a powerful enemy with weaponry far superior to what was available to the nation of Israel—the people were afraid. But instead of turning to and trusting in the Lord once again, they devised a plan of their own. They decided that what they needed to do in order to be victorious was simply to bring the ark of the covenant into battle with them. They reasoned, *"When it comes among us it may save us from the hand of our enemies"* (verse 3).

The problem with their plan was that they were substituting the ark of the covenant for the Presence of the Lord, and in doing so they were clinging to the shadow instead of the substance. The ark of the covenant contained:

- The tablets of the law (representing His guidance).

- Aaron's rod that budded (representing His leadership).

- A jar of manna from the days in the wilderness (representing His provision).

- The golden mercy seat (representing His dwelling place).

Indeed, the ark of the covenant represented God, but it did not contain Him. The ark was the most holy of all the furnishings in the tabernacle, but it was not God. The people mistakenly entrusted a mere symbol to give them victory, and saddest of all, they did not even know that the Presence of God was not with them until it was too late. They let religious symbols and traditions take the place of a real relationship with the Lord, and this gave them a false sense of security.

BE A BEREAN

Religion can never take the place of a personal relationship with the Lord. We cannot carry symbols of God around, recite rote prayers to Him, practice dead traditions, or deny the work of the Holy Spirit, and then expect that His power and victory will be evident in our lives. Religious rituals and emblems may give us confidence while we are in the camp, but there is no real victory in the battlefield beyond. The Israelites paid a large price for their presumption. They suffered a huge defeat in the battle. Many lives were lost and the ark was captured and taken away by their enemy—all because they trusted in the outward emblems of their faith rather than cultivating hearts that truly sought after God.

Romans 15:4 says, *"Whatever things were written before were written for our learning, that we through the patience and comfort of the Scriptures might have hope."* The lesson we need to learn is that the victorious Christian life is a byproduct of our personal relationship with God. When we satisfy ourselves with anything less than that, we are deceiving ourselves. We are setting up idols in our own hearts, and God will allow defeat in our lives in order to reveal the emptiness of what we have placed our trust in. Emotional experiences and man-made traditions, no matter how supernatural or pious they may appear, are not on an equal par with the divinely inspired Word of God.

Satan really has done a number on the people of God. He has no problem with us embracing all kinds of religious experiences, or debating every doctrinal theory or spiritual "hobbyhorse" that comes around. He has filled our lives with all sorts of distractions in order to keep us from understanding the real position we have been given in Christ and the real power we have received in the Holy Spirit. Satan is not threatened by our religious activities. It is only those whose lives are yielded to, filled with, and empowered by the Holy Spirit that pose any threat to his work at all.

We should not blindly follow any teaching that does not line up with the teaching of Scripture.

Ultimately each of us is responsible for how we live our Christian life. We are told to *"work out [our] own salvation with fear and trembling"* (Philippians 2:12). We need to become familiar with the real truth of the gospel so that we are able to detect a counterfeit when we see one. In summary, what we need is the Word of God working on the outside, together with the Spirit of God working on the inside. Then we will have wisdom and we will know the difference between truth and error.

The bottom line is that we should not blindly follow any teaching that does not line up with the teaching of Scripture. In Acts, Paul commended the noble-minded people of Berea for this very thing. He said, *"They received the word with all readiness, and searched the Scriptures daily to find out whether these things were so"* (Acts 17:11). They did not just take Paul at his word. They checked what he was saying with what the Scriptures taught. We ought to do the same. Only in this way can we be sure that we will not be led astray.

All Scripture is given by inspiration of God, and is profitable for doctrine, for reproof, for correction, for instruction in righteousness, that the man of God may be complete, thoroughly equipped for every good work.

—2 TIMOTHY 3:16–17

Chapter Six Study Guide

TEST ALL THINGS

◆　◆　◆

1. In the opening paragraphs of this chapter, it is stated that "the confusion that exists today within the body of Christ is proof that Satan's strategy to prevent Christians from understanding what the Bible says about the Holy Spirit's rightful place in their lives has been a huge success." In what ways have you seen Satan use confusion and division in relation to the power of the Holy Spirit in the church today?

_____

_____

_____

2. What are the two extreme viewpoints on how the Holy Spirit manifests Himself that are widely held in the church today? Can you give an example of each?

a. _____

_____

b. _____

_____

3. How can we test to see if an experience is a true work of the Holy Spirit? Give two examples.

a. _____

_____

b. _____

_____

4. What is one of the surest marks of a genuine encounter with the Holy Spirit?

_____

_____

5. Fill in the missing words from this quote from the chapter.

"Genuine humility makes way for both the _____ and _____ of God to be manifested _____, and known _____, our lives."

6. Reflect on the Andrew Murray quote found in this chapter:

"We want to get possession of the power and use it. God wants the power to get possession of us and use us."

_____

_____

a. What does this mean to you personally, and how does it change your understanding of the relationship between you and the Holy Spirit?

_____

_____

7. What are the three proofs given in this chapter that the gifts of the Spirit are still in operation today?

a. _____

_____

b. _____

_____

c. _____

_____

8. What is the danger of the viewpoint that God's gifts are not in existence today?

_____

_____

9. How can we be sure that we will not be led astray by false teaching?

_____

_____

As you close out this time of study, take a few moments and ask the Lord to give you discernment in all things, and the wisdom to know the difference between truth and error. (Read Philippians 1:9–11.)

After the initial excitement and tremendous joy over our salvation ebbs away a little, we make an amazing discovery: God isn't satisfied yet with what we look like! We learn from His word that, "God didn't create man to tend His garden, and He didn't save us to have workers for His harvest field. God's original and sole purpose for man has always been to manifest His image." That's what He is after when He begins to deal with our human nature. . . . God actually expects His children to possess the same kind of deep humility and total submission that Jesus had, so that we too will have rivers of living water flow from our lives to this dying world.[1]

—*K. P. Yohannan*

True Knowledge of Jesus

"When the Helper comes, whom I shall send to you from the Father, the Spirit of truth who proceeds from the Father, He will testify of Me. And you will also bear witness . . ."

—JOHN 15:26–27

All the work of the Holy Spirit centers on Jesus Christ: He testifies of Him. In the preceding chapters we learned many ways that we can tell whether our lives are yielded to the Holy Spirit. However, the greatest evidence that we are yielded to the Holy Spirit is that Jesus will be at the center of our lives and at the center of everything we do. So when we are under the influence of the Holy Spirit, our lives will also be testimonies of who Jesus is.

I heard a good illustration of this point recently. A number of well-known Bible teachers were brought in to speak to a group of eager and bright students at a Bible college. On the first night the students were awed by a popular preacher who spoke eloquently, using a number of great illustrations and anecdotes to punctuate his main points. The students stayed up late that night wondering where he had gotten all those great stories and powerful illustrations.

The next night, the students heard from another well-known speaker. This man was an excellent exegetical Bible teacher with a vast knowledge of the Hebrew and Greek languages. He impressed them as he expounded upon almost every word, exposing shades of meaning that were lost in the translation. Afterward, the students once again talked into the early morning hours, each of them determining to spend more time studying their lexicons.

The students were treated to another notable speaker on the following night. This man spoke simply, but with great power, of Jesus Christ and the enormity of His love toward us. The reality of his devotion to his Lord was evident to all in attendance. The students stayed up late again that night talking, only this time their conversation was not centered on a man or on his methods, but on the Lord and on His incredible love for them. The fragrance that night was distinctly Christ, and bore testimony to the hearts of each one of those students of who Jesus is.

One of the ways we know that the Holy Spirit is at work is that He will always bear witness of Jesus. He will always bring the testimony of Christ's life into our hearts. R. A. Torrey wrote:

> No amount of listening to the testimony of men regarding Jesus Christ, and no amount even of studying what the Scriptures say about Christ, will ever lead anyone to the knowledge of Jesus Christ unless the Holy Spirit, the living Spirit of God, takes the message of men, or the testimony of the written Word, and interprets it directly to our hearts.[2]

Every Christian has received an incredible blessing in the Person of the Holy Spirit; we have received the true knowledge of Jesus Christ.

THE POVERTY OF IGNORANCE

Jesus came to give us life and that *"more abundantly"* (John 10:10). The "normal" Christian experience, therefore, should be a spiritually rich one filled with adventure, purpose, power, joy, and holiness. Yet, as I talk with Christians I find that very often they are not living this kind of life. They simply do not seem to understand, and as a result, cannot apprehend the new life they have been given in Christ. The words spoken through the prophet Hosea, *"My people are destroyed for lack of knowledge"* (Hosea 4:6), are a much-needed exhortation in the church today. Too many of us are living as paupers in the presence of our King, choosing the poverty of self-rule over the abundant Spirit-filled life that is the inheritance of every Christian.

Poverty, no matter how you view it, is always tragic. Perhaps you have seen pictures or even had the opportunity to visit regions where people live in great distress due to its devastation. Those born into such hopelessness oftentimes live their whole lives in the confines of its cruel prison, all because of one thing: lack—they lack the power necessary to effectively change their circumstances. And while you may be tempted to think that there is no greater hopelessness in this world than to be bound by abject poverty, there really is something far worse: the poverty brought on by our own ignorance. A person whose poverty is a direct result of his or her own ignorance is in the most hopeless of all situations. After all, what more can be done for someone who already has everything they need, but does not utilize the resources that they have been given?

> An old Scottish woman lived in the most impoverished conditions. Years before, her son had immigrated to America. There he had become a very successful businessman, but never found time to return home to visit his mother. One day a friend sat talking with the old lady in her sparsely furnished cottage. "Doesn't your son ever send you any money to help with your needs?" she inquired.
>
> "No," the woman shook her head sadly. "He does write me nice letters, though. And he sends me the most interesting pictures!"
>
> The listener was annoyed, because she knew that the son was quite wealthy. But instead of speaking

her mind, she simply said, "May I see the pictures?" The aged mother proudly brought them out of a drawer. To her visitor's amazement, they were not pictures at all. They were valuable bank notes from America amounting to thousands of dollars.

For years, this woman had been needlessly living in poverty. The problem? She did not know the value of those "interesting pictures." She owned the notes, but she had not taken full possession of them. Her poverty was not due to the fact that she lacked wealth. The money her son had sent from America was available to meet all her needs, but she left those resources sitting in a drawer untapped because she did not know the purpose, or value, of the precious gift that she had received. Her own ignorance had brought needless suffering and sorrow into her life.

Most people today are not as foolish when it comes to understanding the value of money as this poor woman. Her experience is definitely not a common one. As a matter of fact, when we read this story we have a hard time comprehending how anyone could ever wind up in this kind of self-imposed poverty. But this is all too common among Christians. A great deal of self-imposed "spiritual poverty" exists in the church today. I would even say that it is epidemic among those who call themselves believers.

According to surveys conducted recently by the Barna Research Group, only half of the adults who identified themselves as Christians said that they were absolutely committed to their Christian faith.[3] That is astounding, because unless you are absolutely committed to the Christian faith, you really have not embraced it at all. So, half of all those who say they are Christians probably are not. In addition, their research showed that among those who say they are born-again believers:

84 percent believe the Bible is totally accurate

50 percent believe Satan is just a symbol of evil and not a real living being

38 percent believe you can earn a place in heaven by being good enough

32 percent believe in moral absolutes (right and wrong)

31 percent believe Jesus sinned just like the rest of us

26 percent think that all religions are the same

15 percent do not believe in the bodily resurrection of Christ [4]

This is a sad commentary on modern Christianity. It reveals that Christians, by and large, do not really understand the incredible wealth that has been credited to their accounts. They are just like the old Scottish woman who, because of her ignorance, never utilized what was at her disposal. They count the promises of God as merely "interesting words," and in ignorance they disregard the riches of Christ. They forget that God is alive and active today, and as a result they wind up living bankrupt Christian lives, while leaving a wealth of spiritual resources untapped.

There is no greater tragedy than the poverty of trying to live the Christian life apart from the empowerment of the Holy Spirit.

So many Christians believe in the God of history and the God of prophecy; we believe all the great things He did in Wesley's day and in Moody's day. We believe in the great things He is going to do when He comes again. But how few of His people really believe that He is the God of today, that He is a present, living power in our hearts![5]

—*Alan Redpath*

As tragic as poverty is in this world, there is no greater tragedy than the poverty of trying to live the Christian life apart from the empowerment of the Holy Spirit. Yet, this is the kind of poverty that many Christians are enslaved in today. I know this very well myself, because I lived in that poverty for many years. The church I grew up in was so afraid of being labeled fanatical that we never even heard about the Holy Spirit. We learned all about what was expected of us as Christians, but nothing about the empowerment available to live as He desires. As a result, after trying really hard to be a "good" Christian, I gave up. I was just not able to do it in my own strength—I could not understand how anyone could really live up to the standard of holiness that was expected.

Unfortunately, my early Christian experience was not an unusual one. Many believers today are also trying to live the Christian life in the power of the flesh. What we need to understand is that trying to live as a Christian by simply reforming our old nature is about as effective as trying to shore up the foundations of an old building by slapping on a fresh coat of paint. It may look good on the outside for a little while, but eventually the rottenness will surface and the façade will crack once again. Just like an old sagging structure whose rotted beams need replacing, so too our old nature needs to be replaced because it is hopelessly corrupt. Nothing we can do—no amount of self-help books or graduate degrees—will ever change that fact. Only Jesus' life in us changes anything, and that "river of life" only flows through yielded human vessels!

> "For all those things My hand has made, and all those things exist," says the LORD. "But on this one will I look: on him who is poor and of a contrite spirit, and who trembles at My word."
>
> —ISAIAH 66:2

A LIFE OF PERFECT SUBMISSION

In His humanity, Jesus gave us the blueprint for Christian living—He was perfectly yielded to the Father's will and plan for His life. Jesus remained totally dependent upon the power of the Holy Spirit in order to carry out that plan. He never used His own authority as

God while living among us as a man, even though He could have. On the night He was arrested Jesus rebuked Peter for drawing his sword, saying, *"Do you think that I cannot now pray to My Father, and He will provide Me with more than twelve legions of angels?"* (Matthew 26:53).

Jesus did not surrender His divinity when He came to earth, but out of obedience to His Father and because of His incredible passion for us, He chose to experience everything that we go through: every temptation, every sorrow, every pain, every weakness. Hebrews 4:15 reminds us, *"For we do not have a High Priest who cannot sympathize with our weaknesses, but was in all points tempted as we are, yet without sin."* Jesus completely identified with us in our humanity so that we could experience His life through the gift of salvation.

> [Jesus], being in the form of God, did not consider it robbery to be equal with God, but made Himself of no reputation, taking the form of a bondservant, and coming in the likeness of men. And being found in appearance as a man, He humbled Himself and became obedient to the point of death, even the death of the cross.
>
> —PHILIPPIANS 2:6–8

The evidence of His love toward us was fully demonstrated at the cross. Jesus, despite the power and authority He had to overcome His enemies and free Himself from their shackles, chose rather to submit Himself to their brutality. *"I gave My back to those who struck Me, and My cheeks to those who plucked out the beard; I did not hide My face from shame and spitting"* (Isaiah 50:6).

Consider the reality of this for a moment. Suppose that you had Jesus' power and were able to call legions of angels to aid you in a difficult circumstance. Although nothing you or I face could ever compare to what Jesus suffered, it would be very tempting for us indeed to use the kind of power that He possessed for our own benefit. In my life, I know that even the most minor inconveniences, such as driving behind someone who is really slow, causes me to want to take action. If I had the power to beam some of those cars right into the next lane, it would be very tempting indeed. Yet despite the cruelty, pain, and injustice of the cross, Jesus never flinched. He never argued. Instead He laid His will down, and Scripture says He *"opened not His mouth"* (Isaiah 53:7).

> True humility is the silence of the soul before God,
> when a person ceases to argue or debate but rests in
> His Word.[6]
>
> —*Alan Redpath*

Living the Christian life, therefore, is not our *responsibility,* as much as it is our *response to His ability.*

In Jesus' life, we see a beautiful picture of what it means to be a yielded servant. His life also reveals to us (with more clarity than ever before) the hopelessness of our situation apart from Him. How can we, being full of selfishness, greed, pride, arrogance, and every other "natural" human trait ever hope to reflect the image of Christ in our world? The key is that we need to fix our gaze upon Jesus, and take our eyes off everything else—He is the *"author and finisher of our faith"* (Hebrews 12:2). And the Holy Spirit bears witness of the reality and power of Christ's life. Only by yielding to Him will we be able to live the powerful and purpose-filled life we were intended to live. Only in humbling ourselves and receiving from Him will we be able to truly live for Him. Living the Christian life, therefore, is not our *responsibility,* as much as it is our *response to His ability.*

> He [Jesus] is the one who is at work in us to help us
> want to do his will and then to help even more as we
> try to do it. We are his workmanship. What we are is
> his full responsibility and he accepts it. Our job is to
> stay on the same team as he, cast our cares on him,

and let him do the scoring against Satan for us: "The one who is in you is greater than the one who is in the world" (1 John 4:4).[7]

—Gayle Erwin

In Christ, the God of heaven emptied Himself and put on a cloak of flesh. He walked as a man and was empowered by the Holy Spirit who was upon Him. His life is, therefore, a perfect example to us of the yielded life. He did nothing of Himself, but in all things He was in complete submission to the will of the Father: the places He went, the words He spoke, and the miracles He performed. The power He demonstrated in His life was also perfect. He taught with authority, fully engaging the culture. He never thought of Himself, but was full of compassion for the lost. He caused the blind to see, the deaf to hear, the lame to walk, and the dead to rise. He fed the hungry and promised an endless supply of life-giving water to those who were thirsty. And He told His disciples that they would do even greater things than these when the Holy Spirit came upon them. The Holy Spirit enables us to live the Christian life by keeping our eyes focused on the only One who can—Jesus.

FOCUSED ON JESUS

In the Old Testament, the Lord gave specific instructions to His people in the building of the altar. They were told to fashion it from plain, uncut stones. The altar was to be simple, not displaying anyone's handiwork, so that the people's attention would not be distracted from the sacrifice it held. Likewise, as the church gathers together today, nothing should be distracting our attention from Jesus—God's perfect sacrifice. Yet, how easy it is for us to get distracted. Professionalism has crept into many church services, shifting the focus off the "sacrifice," and onto the "altar." If we hear well-crafted messages, but the gospel is not preached, if we sing great songs, but the Lord is not worshiped, if we see beautiful decorations, but we see nothing of Jesus, then the focus is not on Christ and Him crucified. It is not on the sacrifice, it is on the altar.

Paul told the Corinthians:

> And I, brethren, when I came to you, did not come with excellence of speech or of wisdom declaring to you the testimony of God. For I determined not to know anything among you except Jesus Christ and Him crucified. I was with you in weakness, in fear, and in much trembling. And my speech and my preaching were not with persuasive words of human wisdom, but in demonstration of the Spirit and of power, that your faith should not be in the wisdom of men but in the power of God.
>
> —1 CORINTHIANS 2:1–5

The true nature of the Christian life is not about us being outwardly perfected, but rather inwardly yielded to the One who is—Jesus.

Walking with Jesus is so simple; it requires no great ability. Paul had one agenda—Jesus Christ and Him crucified. With the Lord, it is not about our oratory skills or any of our other fine abilities; it is about Jesus only. That is the message God wants delivered today, and when we depend on the power of the Holy Spirit to help us, God will use our lives to be witnesses of Him.

Like the apostle Paul, God wants to use us even in weakness, fear, and trembling. He seldom calls the qualified, but He always qualifies the called. He has given us the Holy Spirit to enable us to boldly proclaim Jesus in our generation. So we need to examine whose ability we are trusting because the true nature of the Christian life is not about us being outwardly perfected, but rather inwardly yielded to the One who is—Jesus. It is about us submitting to His authority in every area of our lives.

When Jesus was arrested and crucified, the apostles went into hiding. They did not have the courage to live openly for Christ, but when the Holy Spirit was poured out upon them on the day of Pentecost (see Acts 2), a dramatic change occurred in the way they lived their lives from that point on. They had the power to be His witnesses and they lived boldly for Christ even in the face of death because the Holy Spirit had come upon them.

Jesus said that all who believed in Him would receive this same power. He did not promise to strengthen our flesh (we too will experience weakness, fear, and trembling); He promised to give us a new Spirit. That is why we need to ask the Spirit of God to come upon us in all His power and with all His resources and enable us to live as witnesses of Christ in our generation.

> It is no longer I who live, but Christ lives in me; and the life which I now live in the flesh I live by faith in the Son of God.
>
> —GALATIANS 2:20

FREEDOM IN CHRIST

The greatest fulfillment, happiness, and peace that we will ever experience as Christians comes from knowing the freedom we have in Christ. What we believe about ourselves and about God makes a big difference in the way we live. So let me ask you: How free are you today? Do you realize the inheritance that is yours in Christ? In Him we have been set free from:

- The condemnation of sin—death!

  For the wages of sin is death, but the gift of God is eternal life in Christ Jesus our Lord. (Romans 6:23)

- The power of Satan!

  The Son of God was manifested, that He might destroy the works of the devil. (1 John 3:8)

- The control of our sinful nature!

Reckon yourselves to be dead indeed to sin, but alive to God in Christ Jesus our Lord. (Romans 6:11)

- The pressure to conform to the world!

He who is in you is greater than he who is in the world. (1 John 4:4)

Do you understand the power that is already *in* you—the power to overcome that smoking habit, get a handle on your temper, or to break off that ungodly relationship? Do you realize that you have already been totally set free? Power and freedom are yours in Christ today! That is the truth of who you are in Him. The question is: Do you know and are you walking in it?

> The Holy Spirit within is the One who is coaxing us, each day, to step into the newness of life we have in Christ.

Some friends told me once about something unexpected that happened when they were housebreaking a little puppy. In order to train him, they first kept him confined in a small, fenced-off area. Once he was fully housebroken, however, they removed the bars that had kept him from roaming freely about, and gave the puppy complete access to the whole house. The funny thing was that the little puppy would not leave that one small area. Even though the bars were gone, his freedom was still restricted. They did everything to try and coax him into the rest of the house, but he would not venture beyond the area where they had first kept him. Freedom was his, yet he was still in bondage.

Many Christians are living like this little puppy. Jesus has opened the prison door, yet they remain confined and afraid to venture out into the freedom that His life has wrought for them. The Holy Spirit within is the One who is coaxing us, each day, to step into the newness of life we have in Christ. He desires for us to take full possession of all that we have been given. There is no reason why we should remain imprisoned and shackled to sin any longer: Jesus has set the captives free!

I have never regretted the decision I made in college to live fully for Christ. At the time, I remember my friends thought that this was just another passing fad that I had latched onto, but it was more than that—it was a real change. Today, I can testify that the promises God has made in His Word are being fulfilled daily in my life through the indwelling power of the Holy Spirit. As Isaiah 58:11 says, He has indeed guided me continually, He has satisfied my soul in times of drought, and strengthened my bones. His Presence has made my life like a well-watered garden because His waters never fail.

What about you? What kind of Christian life are you living? Do you have power over sin and temptation? Are others drawn to Christ by the example of your life? Or are you living in self-imposed poverty like the old Scottish woman, ignorant of the riches you have inherited in Christ? Maybe you are like that little puppy, peering out of your prison cell, but afraid to trust fully in the One who gave His life to set you free. If so, I want to challenge you to be more like the early disciples whose lives were dramatically changed because they waited, expectantly, for the power of the Holy Spirit to come upon them.

When slavery was abolished at the end of the Civil War, there were many slaves who did not realize that they had been set free. They kept on living as though they were still in bondage, missing out on experiencing the greatest joy of their new lives. Similarly, once you believed in Jesus, He emancipated you from the bondage of sin. He did for you what you could not do for yourself. I exhort you: Do not miss out on experiencing the greatest joy of your new life in Christ. Be willing to do your part—be willing to live yielded, *Under His Influence.*

> *Give me love that leads the way,*
> *The faith that nothing can dismay,*
> *The hope no disappointments tire,*

The passion that will burn like fire,
Let me not sink to be a clod;
Make me Thy fuel, Flame of God.[8]

—*Amy Carmichael*

Chapter Seven Study Guide

TRUE KNOWLEDGE OF JESUS

◆ ◆ ◆

1. What is the greatest evidence that we are yielded to the Holy Spirit?

_____

_____

2. What should the normal Christian experience look like? Does your life look like your answer? What is missing?

_____

_____

3. What is the primary reason Christians are not experiencing powerful, obedient, and victorious lives?

_____

_____

4. Reflect on how the poverty of ignorance can be related spiritually. In what ways would you say that you might be living a life of spiritual poverty?

_____

_____

5. In this chapter, various statistics were listed bearing witness to the condition of the Christian church. Do any of these startle you?

_____

_____

In light of this, examine your own heart to determine what it is that you believe.

6. Reflect on the statement made in this chapter: "Unless you are absolutely committed to the Christian faith, you have not really embraced it at all." What do you think about this statement?

_____

_____

7. What is the two-part blueprint Jesus gave us for Christian living?

   a. _____

   _____

   b. _____

   _____

8. The following is a quote from this chapter. Fill in the missing words.

   "Living the Christian life, therefore, is not our _____, as much as it is our _____ to His _____."

9. We are told that by observing Jesus we learn how to live the Christian life. Reflect and write of one gospel account or one Scripture about Jesus that you would like to have lived out in your life. Give a scriptural reference if you can.

_____

_____

_____

10. After Jesus' death the apostles went into hiding because they did not have the courage to live openly for Christ. What happened on the day of Pentecost that changed everything?

_____

_____

11. What were some of the changes that occurred in them after that day?

_____

_____

12. How about you? Have you seen this kind of power displayed in your life?

_____

_____

13. Are you living a life of self-imposed poverty because you were never aware of the riches that are available to you as a believer?

_____

_____

14. List the four areas where we have been set free in Christ:

a. _____

_____

b. _____

_____

c. _____

_____

d. _____

_____

15. Have you been set free in these areas? Do you realize that this is your inheritance?

_____

_____

16. Look back at your answer to the first question in the *Introduction.* Have your objectives in reading this book been fulfilled?

_____

_____

17. What new insights or understanding have you gained and how do you plan to put them into practice? Remember it isn't your responsibility, but your response to His ability.

_____

_____

As we close this Bible study, ask God to help you live a submitted and yielded life, *Under His Influence.*

NOTES

CHAPTER ONE

[1] Gordon, S. D. *Quiet Talks on Power.* Third Edition. Grand Rapids, MI: Fleming H. Revell (n.d.).

[2] Spurgeon, C. H. *What the Holy Spirit Does in a Believer's Life.* Seattle, WA: YWAM Publishing, 1996.

[3] Moody, D. L. Source unknown.

[4] Habershon, Ada R. "I Need to Be Filled." Posted July 24, 2004. *The Cyber Hymnal. www.cyberhymnal.org.* (Accessed October 15, 2004.)

CHAPTER TWO

[1] Sanders, J. Oswald. *The Holy Spirit and His Gifts.* Grand Rapids, MI: Zondervan Publishing, 1940.

[2] Harvey, Edwin and Lillian. *Royal Insignia.* Hampton, TN: Harvey Christian Publishers, 2000.

[3] Tozer, A. W. Source unknown.

[4] Graham, Billy. *The Holy Spirit.* Dallas, TX: Word Publishing, 1988.

[5] Choy, Leona Frances. *Powerlines: What Great Evangelicals Believed About the Holy Spirit, 1850–1930.* Camp Hill, PA: Christian Publications, 1990.

CHAPTER THREE

[1] Simpson, A. B. *Christ in the Tabernacle.* Camp Hill, PA: Christian Publications, 1985.

[2] Murray, Andrew. *Revival.* Minneapolis, MN: Bethany House, 1990.

[3] Simpson, A. B. Source unknown.

[4] Meyer, F. B. *Fit for the Master's Use.* Santa Ana, CA: Calvary Chapel Publishing, 2002.

[5] Graham, Billy. *The Holy Spirit.* Dallas, TX: Word Publishing, 1988.

[6] "Evan Roberts." Posted July 6, 2003. *UCB Online. www.welshrevival.com.* (Accessed October 13, 2004.)

CHAPTER FOUR

[1] Redpath, Alan. *The Making of a Man of God: Studies in the Life of David.* Grand Rapids, MI: Fleming H. Revell, 1994.

[2] Sanders, J. Oswald. *The Holy Spirit and His Gifts.* Grand Rapids, MI: Zondervan Publishing, 1981.

[3] Ibid.

[4] Begbie, Harold. "The Life of General William Booth." Posted 2002. *The Salvation Army.* www.uss.salvationarmy.org. (Accessed October 13, 2004.)

CHAPTER FIVE

[1] Smith, Chuck. *Living Water.* Eugene, OR: Harvest House Publishers, 1996.

[2] Chambers, Oswald. *My Utmost for His Highest.* Grand Rapids, MI: Discovery House Publishers, 1992.

[3] Smith, Chuck. *Charisma vs. Charismania.* Costa Mesa, CA: The Word For Today, 2000.

[4] Ibid.

[5] Monod, Theodore. "O the Bitter Shame and Sorrow." Posted June 30, 2004. *The Cyber Hymnal.* www.cyberhymnal.org. (Accessed October 15, 2004.)

CHAPTER SIX

[1] Lockyer, Herbert. *All About the Holy Spirit.* Peabody, MA: Hendrickson Publishers, 1995.

[2] Smith, Chuck. *Living Water.* Eugene, OR: Harvest House Publishers, 1996.

[3] Lockyer, Herbert. *All About the Holy Spirit.* Peabody, MA: Hendrickson Publishers, 1995.

[4] Murray, Andrew. *Humility.* New Kensington, PA: Whitaker House, 1982.

[5] Grubb, Norman. *Rees Howells: Intercessor.* Fort Washington, PA: Christian Literature Crusade, 1999.

[6] Murray, Andrew. *The Spirit of Christ.* Bloomington, MN: Bethany Fellowship Inc., 1979.

[7] Spurgeon, C. H. *Lectures to My Students.* Grand Rapids, MI: Zondervan Publishing, 1954.

CHAPTER SEVEN

[1] Yohannan, K. P. *Reflecting His Image.* Carrollton, TX: GFA Books, 1998.

[2] Wubbles, Lance, ed. *R. A. Torrey on the Holy Spirit.* Lynwood, WA: Emerald Books, 1998.

[3] "The Barna Update." Posted March 19, 2004. *The Barna Group. www.barna.org.* (Accessed October 14, 2004.)

[4] "Born Again Christians." *The Barna Group. www.barna.org.* (Accessed October 14, 2004.)

[5] Redpath, Alan. *The Making of a Man of God: Studies in the Life of David.* Grand Rapids, MI: Fleming H. Revell, 1994.

[6] Ibid.

[7] Erwin, Gayle. *The Jesus Style.* Palm Springs, CA: Ronald N. Haynes Publishers, 1983.

[8] Elliot, Elisabeth. *A Chance to Die: The Life and Legacy of Amy Carmichael.* Grand Rapids, MI: Fleming H. Revell, 1987.

RECOMMENDED READING

THE HOLY SPIRIT AND HIS GIFTS

Edman, V. Raymond. *They Found the Secret*
Erwin, Gayle. *The Spirit Style*
Goforth, Jonathan. *By My Spirit*
Graham, Billy. *The Holy Spirit*
Lockyer, Herbert. *All About the Holy Spirit*
Moody, D. L. *Secret Power*
Smith, Chuck. *Charisma vs. Charismania*
Smith, Chuck. *Living Water*
Spurgeon, C. H. *Power for You*
Spurgeon, C. H. *What the Holy Spirit Does in a Believer's Life*
Torrey, R. A. *The Baptism with the Holy Spirit*
Tozer, A. W. *How to Be Filled with the Holy Spirit*

THE YIELDED LIFE

Francis, R. Mabel. *Filled With the Spirit . . . Then What?*
Hession, Roy. *The Calvary Road*
Meyer, F. B. *Fit for the Master's Use*
Munger, Robert Boyd. *My Heart, Christ's Home*
Murray, Andrew. *Abide in Christ*
Murray, Andrew. *Absolute Surrender*
Murray, Andrew. *Waiting on God*
Sanders, J. Oswald. *Christ Indwelling and Enthroned*

DEVOTIONALS

Chambers, Oswald. *My Utmost for His Highest*
Harvey, E. F. and L. *Kneeling We Triumph*
Murray, Andrew. *The Path to Holiness*
Yohannan, K. P. *Reflecting His Image*

OTHER MATERIALS AVAILABLE BY PASTOR LLOYD

PATIENT EVANGELISM: REACHING THE MULTITUDES ONE AT A TIME

Do you want to impact your world the way that Jesus did? In this book, Pastor Lloyd shares some practical ways that will enable you to follow the Lord's example when sharing your faith with those around you.

THE HOLY SPIRIT SERIES

The Word of God promises that the Holy Spirit helps in our weaknesses. Join Pastor Lloyd as he explores the Holy Spirit's place in our lives and the various gifts of the Spirit. (Available in audiocassette, CD, and MP3 format.)

REVIVAL!

What the church needs today is revival. Join Pastor Lloyd as he explores the topic of revival throughout the pages of Scripture and the annals of church history, and discover how you can experience personal revival through the power of the Lord. (Available in audiocassette, CD, and MP3 format.)

Visit Calvary Chapel Old Bridge's website at www.ccob.org if you want to order any of these resources, or if you wish to receive additional information and audio messages by Pastor Lloyd Pulley. Video/audiotape, CD packages, and Bible studies are also available online. You may also contact us by calling 732-679-9222 or by writing to:

Calvary Chapel Old Bridge
123 White Oak Lane
Old Bridge, NJ 08857